Grow or I
By I

MW00827712

ISOB - Grow or Die-Seminar Series - ver. 6.2

First Printing - March, 1999 - version 5.5
Second printing - August, 1999 version 5.6
Third printing, 2002 version 5.7 - French
Fourth printing 2005 version 5.7 Spanish
Fifth printing 2005 version 6.0 English
Sixth printing version 6.2 2006 English

Grow or Die is published by and is a discipleship curriculum of the
International School of The Bible
Marietta, GA USA
Email address growordie@isob-bible.org -www.isob-bible.org
ISBN # 0-9676731-3-5
978-0-9676731-3-4

The theme of Grow or Die

Path to Grow.. ⟶

Fruit for
character
personal needs
ministry

Flowing River - In living fellowship with God	Who God is	SIT His Cross	WALK Your cross	STAND Warfare

Satan defeated

..or Die

Stuck in defeat, a prisoner in the promise land.	Ha, I win!

Table of Contents

Dear Reader:

After passionately following Jesus since 1979, He has commissioned me to document the process that He has taken me through time and time again. While there are no short cuts in bearing fruit, or in developing your relationship with Jesus, and there are many things that you just experience for yourself, there are principles that I have learned that could take years of pain and discouragement off of your life.

This book contains a short version of Grow or Die called the "Seminar Series." It consists of two seminars. The first seminar (Section 1) consists of the seven "lead lessons." The second seminar (Section 2) consists of four follow up lessons. These 11 lessons are extracted from the full Grow or die course that consists of over 100 lessons.

The entire Grow or Die course is available for individuals and/or groups for discipleship.

Some groups have organized into ISOB mentoring schools (in several countries around the world). Some groups are using the materials for group study as they meet. Individuals are doing self-study in many cases.

Others have seen the Lord start a church-planting ministry as a result of leaders being built up and bearing fruit through this curriculum.

Grow or Die is currently being presented as a seminar for Gospel workers in several countries. The seminars range from 4 hours to 14 hours.

ISOB does not charge for any of its materials beyond the costs of reproduction. The lessons are available on CD ROM for Windows and Apple computers.

In addition to Grow or Die, ISOB has books, videos and CDs for ISOB Bondage Breakers, a series for breaking strongholds and addictions. We have a marriage series and other valuable disciples books and lessons.

We bless you in your adventure with Jesus,

Larry Chkoreff
President
International School of The Bible – 1999 –updated 2006

This book is dedicated to my two best friends, Jesus and my precious and godly wife Carol, who for years has encouraged me to write these lessons, and finally to assemble them in book form. I am also thankful to the ISOB Partners around the world who, since 1998, have taught these lessons and encouraged me with the fruit of their labor.

This prayer is declared over every person who reads this book.

The Cross. Thank you, Lord Jesus Christ, for the victory of your Cross. Thank you that we were crucified with you.

Hell. Thank you, Lord Jesus Christ, for going into Hell for us and suffering death for us.

Resurrection. Thank you, Lord Jesus Christ, that you were raised from the dead, and that we were raised with you and are seated with you in Heavenly places in Christ.

In-filling. Thank you, Lord Jesus Christ, for filling us with the Holy Spirit.

Suffering. Thank you, Lord Jesus Christ, for considering us worthy to share in the fellowship of your sufferings. Thank you that with your resurrection power we can turn all suffering into a blessing.

Triumph. Thank you, Lord Jesus Christ, for the triumph that you promise us in this life and in eternity.

Introduction

Have you ever felt without purpose, and without hope?

Have you ever felt as if you were on a wheel like a hamster (or a mouse) in a cage, going nowhere? Have you ever wondered how God expects you to make it through this life? You may feel that God will take you to Heaven some day, but you feel that He has just left you to make it on your own while you are in the here and now. Well join the ranks. Even believers in Jesus Christ feel that way from time to time.

Sometimes just trying to make life work for ourselves seems to be our purpose. For the mother that means raising her children in Godliness, feeding and caring for them. For the wife it means looking for intimacy and emotional security with her husband, a true two-way relationship. For the man it often means trying to provide for his family and trying to find some significance in his life; he wants to be admired. To the young person it may mean finding his/her place in life, his/her occupation and spouse. So often overcoming life's problems seem to become our purpose. However, when these work out we often feel empty and without further purpose, or if they do not work out we feel discouraged and hopeless.

What is the answer?

If we are, as Galatians 2:20 says, crucified with Christ, and Christ is living His life in us, then we are not going to feel right unless our purpose is God's purpose. Yielding to Him completely, and asking Him to make His purpose your purpose is the only thing that will bring peace to your life.

I believe that God has many purposes for us and for this life. However I feel that they all come under the heading of one major purpose, the primary purpose, which is bringing the Bride to his son Jesus. Certainly God wants to take care of your needs, but we need to focus on God's need. His overall purpose is to be glorified.

You may say, "How does this apply to me?" I can barely survive life, and you are talking about a Bride and glorifying God." Hang on, this applies to you! If you can get your life lined up with God's overall purpose, He will take care of all of your needs.

He has a purpose customized just for your life. He wants you to be whole to have your needs met, physically, emotionally, and spiritually. However He has His own path for accomplishing that, and it revolves around His Bride.

Ephesians gives us some insight. The Body or the Church is His Bride. Jesus is passionate about His Bride the Church.

Ephesians 5:32 talks about the mystery of Christ and the church being similar to a husband and a wife. Ephesians 5:32 says, "This is a profound mystery--but I am talking about Christ and the church."

The marriage of the Lamb to His Bride seems to be one of the culminating events near the end of the Book of Revelation. Revelation 19:7

says, "Let us be glad and rejoice and we will give glory to Him. For the marriage of the Lamb has come, and His wife has prepared herself."

This does not mean that we all need to go to foreign lands and preach in the streets like an evangelist. No, God has gifted each and every one of us in a unique and special way. The work (for bringing the Bride home) that He has for you is suited only for your own individual personality, and only you can do it. You are equally important with every other Christian.

Think of it. If there is just one human being who is supposed to be in the Bride and he/she is not in yet, then the Bride is incomplete. As long as the Bride needs to grow into a mature person, then our job is incomplete.

God may call you to pray, or to love your next-door neighbor, or go to a distant land. He may call you to raise your children in godliness, and to love your spouse. He may call you to overcome the afflictions in your life. Only He knows what He has for you. You can trust Him. However if you allow His purpose to be your purpose, it will eventually contribute to the building up of His Bride, the Church.

We should see ourselves as a grain of sand on the beach. We are not to be noticed, however, without us the beach is incomplete. God needs us to do our part.

Old Testament types give us a look into the heart of God and how He feels about this whole thing.

Eve came from Adam's side. The church came from Christ's side at the Cross.

Look at Genesis 24. Abraham (representing the **Father**) sends his servant (representing the **Holy Spirit** - embodied in you and me) to seek out a bride for his son Isaac (representing **Jesus**).

Genesis 24:4-9 says, "But you shall go to my country and to my kindred, and take a wife to my son Isaac. And the servant said to him, 'Perhaps the woman will not be willing to follow me to this land. Must I necessarily bring your son again to the land from which you came?' And Abraham said to him, 'Take care that you do not bring my son there again. The LORD, the God of Heaven, who took me from my father's house and from the land of my kindred, and who spoke to me, and who swore to me, saying, 'To your seed I will give this land:' He shall send His Angel before you. And you shall take a wife to my son from there. And if the woman will not be willing to follow you, then you shall be clear from this oath of mine. Only do not bring my son there again.' And the servant put his hand under the thigh of Abraham his master and swore to him concerning the matter."

You should read the entire account in Genesis 24. The servant finds Rebekah, the one who waters his camels and gives him water when he arrives at his destination. This happens "before he had finished speaking" (vs. 24:15). He was giving God a "fleece," and before he could get the words out of his mouth, Rebekah showed up and fulfilled the fleece.

Genesis 24:64-67 says, "Rebekah also looked up and saw Isaac. She got down from her camel and asked the servant, 'Who is that man in the field coming to meet us?' 'He is my master,' the servant answered. So she took her veil and covered herself. Then the servant told Isaac all he had done. Isaac brought her into the tent of his mother Sarah, and he married Rebekah. So she became his wife, and he loved her; and Isaac was comforted after his mother's death."

What a perfect way to picture the heart of the unseen God! The Father is determined to obtain a wife for his Son.

You may be asking this question. "How in the world does God expect me to participate in the ministry of bringing home the Bride, if I can't even make my life work for myself?" I am glad you asked. That is the whole issue of this book.

We need to learn what kind of servant the Father sent after the Bride.

"He said to the chief servant in his household, the one in charge of all that he had, 'Put your hand under my thigh.'" (Genesis 24:2).

Notice, the Father did not just send out any servant, He sent out the one who was in charge of all he had. Matthew 24 tells us about another servant who was put in charge of all the possessions. Let's see what we can learn from him. Matthew 24:42-51 is the reference.

First, the servant was ready for His Lord to return. This not only means that we should be ready for Jesus to return to earth someday, but also for Him to "return" now, during this life, to check out how we are being faithful with what we have been entrusted.

The servant was faithful. Being faithful in the small things in life is important to God. God is interested in how we handle the daily affairs in our lives. God never gives us more until we handle the little that we already have with faithfulness. We need to be faithful in the practical things and in spiritual things.

The servant was also a giver. He was taking care of others. Matthew 24:46 says, "It will be good for that servant whose master finds him doing so when he returns."

The servant was not treating other people poorly.

The servant was not living like the unbelievers.

The servant was wise. Obviously, this is not referring to the wisdom of the world, but to Godly wisdom. 1 Corinthians 2:6-8 says, "We do, however, speak a message of wisdom among the mature, but not the wisdom of this age or of the rulers of this age, who are coming to nothing. No, we speak of God's secret wisdom, a wisdom that has been hidden and that God destined for our glory before time began. None of the rulers of this age understood it, for if they had, they would not have crucified the Lord of glory."

1 Corinthians 1:23-24 tells us that Christ crucified is wisdom.

I believe, that true wisdom from God is reserved for those who have gone through "a type of death." It is reserved for those who have lost hopes, dreams, family members, position, reputation; the list goes on. It is for those who have made bad decisions in life and are now willing to make Jesus Lord. Wisdom says that the Cross has given you a fresh start; there is now no condemnation (Romans 8:1-2).

Job 28 talks about looking for wisdom. It says that it is not found in the land of the living. It implies that only death has seen it. The Rich Young Ruler in Matthew 19 had too much to trust in so far as the world was concerned.

When you know for sure that the "world system" and your own efforts offers no hope, then you are a candidate for wisdom. If you fall into this category, lift up your head with hope, because you are a candidate for the supernatural intervention of God!

Life can be difficult, but it can be lived out in victory if we always focus on Jesus.

People, ministers, friends, even churches can disappoint us, but Jesus never will. Hebrews 2:8b-9a says that we don't see all things going perfect just yet, but we see Jesus who tasted death for us. When we realize what Jesus did for us and who He is, we fall in love with Him.

When we fall in love with Him, we can get our satisfaction out of knowing that what we are living for is His purpose, and that is pleasing to Him.

The good thing is that while we are going through the process, we are always focused on Jesus, doing things for Jesus, going through trials for Jesus, serving Jesus. While our eyes are on Him, He is our reward. We do not have to focus on changing our character, or on getting our needs met, or even on ministry. We just have to focus on Him and being one with and in union with Him. We see the "amazing grace" of God overtake us. I can tell you from experience, this makes even the tough times in life tolerable and even joyful.

Now we need to learn how the Father treated His servant, and how we can expect God to treat us.

I see the Father allowing this servant to bear fruit in three ways.

1. The fruit of the Spirit. This servant developed godly character.

2. The fruit of having all his needs met. Notice in Genesis 24:10 that the Father gave the servant all he needed for the journey, not only 10 camels, but all the goods he needed.

3. The fruit of ministry. This servant participated in pleasing the Father and the Son by bringing home the Bride.

Here is how God is glorified and at the same time all of our needs are cared for. "By this My Father is glorified, that you bear much fruit; so you will be My disciples" (John 15:8). God is glorified when you bear fruit because it is His power and His Word that causes fruit. Fruit was the original method God had in mind for taking care of His people. Fruit for our lives brings only what He can do, not what we can do with His help!

We wish to point out some themes that you will recognize as you go through this book. The Parable of the Sower is in Mark chapter 4. Mark 4:11 says that *the mystery* of the Kingdom is in the parable. Notice, not *a* mystery, but *the mystery*. *The mystery* is the Word of God planted in a human heart that bears fruit to the Glory of God. It supplies our character, everything we need for life and godliness including our material and social needs, and it supplies our ministry fruit as well.

Matthew 16-17 tells us more about the Kingdom.

In verse 16:21 Jesus tells His disciples about His death and resurrection. That is *His* Cross. We will focus a lot on His Cross and the blood covenant it represents.

Then in verses 16:24-26 Jesus says that we must take up our cross. That is *our* cross. We will focus a lot on taking up our cross as it takes two people to shed blood in order to ratify a blood covenant.

Then in verse 16:28 Jesus told His disciples that some would see the Kingdom even now before they tasted death.

In Matthew 17 Jesus was transfigured and seen in His future glory by His disciples.

After some discussion about Elijah and Moses and building a residence there to stay in the glory, God spoke from Heaven and said, "This is My beloved Son, in whom I am well pleased. Hear Him."

When we see His Cross, and take up our cross, we will see Jesus and hear His Word, which will be planted in our heart as a powerful and living seed to produce Heaven on earth. Glory to God!

It's all about being desperate!

Why then do so many complicate Christianity? Why do so few walk this way and miss the mystery? Why is it sometimes so difficult to convince Christians to do whatever is needed to see Jesus, to take up their cross, to hear the Word, and trust that it will do God's work for their lives and for God's Kingdom?

Jesus gives us a very simple answer. I have seen people all over the world get a hold of this and I have seen people totally miss it. I pray that all who read this will catch it.

In Matthew 19 the Rich Young Ruler confronts Jesus. Jesus knew that he had much to trust in; riches, fame, position, religion, etc. He advised him to give it away if he really wanted life. You know what happened; he refused and Jesus was grieved because He loved him.

Then the disciples got anxious about how could anybody enter the Kingdom. Jesus told them a parable to answer their concerns. Matthew chapter 20 contains a parable about a man who owned a vineyard and went to the market place to hire workers for the harvest.

He hired the first man for one denarius a day. This was for a full day's work. I submit that he hired the strongest and most able of the five men. This was Man #5

At the third hour he returned to hire more help and asked Man #4 to work a partial day and he would pay him fairly.

At the sixth hour he did likewise. Man # 3.

At the ninth hour he did likewise. Man # 2.

At the eleventh hour he returned again. Man # 1.

He asked Man # 1 why he was still there. The man answered, "Because no one would hire us." He went out and worked for one hour.

First, these men were not lazy or they would not have been sitting in the employment agency all day. Most likely this one-hour man was the least able of all. Perhaps he had a physical or mental handicap. I submit that he was the weakest of all. Remember, this parable is about the Kingdom of God and how and when people receive it.

When pay time came, the master called the one-hour man first, Man # 1, and the all day man, Man # 5, last saying, "So the last will be first and the first last. For many are called but few chosen."

The one-hour man received the Kingdom of God in the here and now and brought the Kingdom to earth, as in the Lord's Prayer. Perhaps Man #5 went to Heaven when he died and received the Kingdom at that time. But the one who had nothing else to trust in received it now.

What was the manifestation of receiving it now? If you are a one-hour man, you will trust only in hearing the Word of God while fellowshipping with Jesus to supply everything you need for life and godliness – see 2 Peter 1:2-11. While we ministered this in a Spanish speaking country the group of leaders really got it. They came up with a theme and carried signs reading, "El Hombre una sola hora." The one-hour man! "We are one-hour people," they shouted. Are you desperate enough to call yourself a "one hour person" and shout halleluiah?

At the end of each chapter of this book, please give yourself this quiz:
What is *the mystery* of the Kingdom?
Who gets the Kingdom first?

That is what this book and discipleship process is all about, bearing fruit in our lives for the Kingdom of God for all three of these areas. May you be blessed!

Section 1 - Seminar 1

Chapters 1-7 deal with:

1. Fruit

2. The Flowing River

3. Prisoners in The Promise Land

4. Who God is

5. Sit

6. Walk

7. Stand

Chapter 1
Fruit

Have you ever asked these questions?
How in the world does God expect me to make it in this life? How am I supposed to live? Why don't I have more victory? If God is for me, then why is my life not looking that way? I have heard about God's power, but maybe He just forgot me when He was passing out the power pills. James 2:5 says, "Listen, my dear brothers: Has not God chosen those who are poor in the eyes of the world to be rich in faith and to inherit the kingdom he promised those who love him?" (Definition of poor: destitute of wealth, influence, position, honor, helpless, powerless to accomplish an end, reduced to beggary, begging, asking alms.)

All of us have real needs. The big three are, love, security and significance. Within these, we all have "felt" needs. Some need food and clothing, some need children to come to know God, some need healing in their bodies, and the list goes on.

Our provisions are in His presence.
Philippians 4:19 says, "But my God shall supply all your need according to his riches in glory by Christ Jesus." If God is going to supply all of your need in "glory," then you are going to have to find out where glory is, and get there; otherwise you could be waiting in the wrong place for God to move. If I am waiting at the train station for the bus, I will never catch the bus. I have to find out where the bus station is! Well, we have to find out where glory is. The word "glory," when it applies to God is simply His presence.

We need to get into His presence and hear Him speak His Word to us. His Word becomes a promise and a seed planted in our heart and eventually will bear fruit *if* we take care of the seed properly.

Bearing fruit is what is important to God.
"This is to my Father's glory, that you bear much fruit, showing yourselves to be my disciples" (John 15:8).

We need to re-direct our efforts from whatever we have been doing and concentrate on bearing fruit.

Adam was created for bearing fruit, what about us?
"God blessed them and said to them, 'Be fruitful and increase in number; fill the earth and subdue it. Rule over the fish of the sea and the birds of the air and over every living creature that moves on the ground.' Then God said, 'I give you every seed-bearing plant on the face of the whole earth and every tree that has fruit with seed in it. They will be yours for food'" (Genesis 1:28-29).

Jesus was telling us to change, repent from struggling to get our needs met, and to become fruit bearers. "From that time on Jesus began to preach, 'Repent, for the kingdom of heaven is near'" (Matthew 4:17). That is to turn and change directions. When you do, you will find the Kingdom of God so close that you can take hold of it.

You may ask, what did He mean? Turn from what? What is the Kingdom of God? I believe that we are to turn from the world's way of living life to the Kingdom's way of living life. I believe that this applies to our entire life. I also believe that Jesus was not simply saying to these people, "Stop sinning and repent from your immoral ways." No, Jesus was giving us the plan for living life.

Humans use all the methods of the world system and of their own self sufficiency to get their unmet needs met. Our basic needs are love, security and impact (significance).

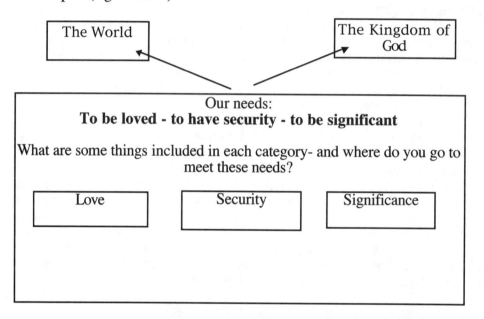

Didn't Peter write that the promises of God provide us with everything we need for life and Godliness? Read 2 Peter 1:3-4.

When they do not get their needs met, people do not want to accept the fact that the world will never provide their needs. They attempt to close the gap by trying to improve themselves, hoping that things will get better. They think there must be something wrong with them. Guilt comes, they misjudge God's character, Satan promotes lies, and they buy these lies. They doubt the truth of God's Word.

So what is the answer?

How do we get the Kingdom of God by turning? Jesus said in Mark 4:11 that *the mystery* of the Kingdom of God is revealed in the parable of sowing and reaping. Sowing and reaping what? Sowing and reaping the Word of God!

The end result of farming is fruit.

Jesus said in Mark 4 that the entire Kingdom of God worked on this principle. He said that this is *the mystery* of the Kingdom. What is the *mystery*? That life is sustained by the Word of God planted in a human heart. The process of growth then takes place. Along with the growth is pain. The pain that results from Satan attempting to steal the Word while you are waiting for the "Lord to return" with the fruit.

He is saying that we need to become Word-dependent people and neither self-dependent, nor world dependent. The way to depend upon God is to depend upon the supernatural power of the Word of God!

We do not need to become so skillful in handling life, as we need to become skillful in handling the Word of God.

Another way to put it is; repent (i.e. take a shift in what you ultimately trust in and depend upon for your most critical need, shift from depending upon yourself and the world system) because the Kingdom of God (i.e., God's system described in Mark 4 of planting the seed of the Word of God in your heart, and allowing it to grow to produce everything you need for life and Godliness, for bearing fruit for God's glory) is now within your reach.

Allow God's grace to take over your life.

Seek ye first the Kingdom of God and His righteousness, and all the things you need will be added to you, they will overtake you like fruit overtakes the branch on the vine (Matthew 6:33).

Acts 26:18 says that when we turn, or repent, we take ourselves out of the power of Satan and put ourselves under the power of God.

There are three kinds of fruit, one for everything we need and everything God needs.

1. Fruit of the Spirit. Interior fruit. This is godly character. This is the fruit that makes you like Jesus. Read Galatians 5:22-23. "But the fruit of the Spirit is love, joy, peace, patience, kindness, goodness, faithfulness, gentleness and self-control. Against such things there is no law."

2. Fruit for our lives. This includes our social, family, health and body, financial, etc. This goes along with 3 John 1:2 that says, "Beloved, I wish above all things that thou mayest prosper and be in health, even as thy soul prospereth." I have experienced more of my needs cared for as my character changed. Read 1 Corinthians 9:7. Who serves as a soldier at his own expense? Who plants a vineyard and does not eat of its grapes? Who tends a flock and does not drink of the milk? John 4:36 says, "Even now the reaper draws his wages, even now he harvests the crop for eternal life, so that the sower and the reaper may be glad together."

A personal testimony.

There was a time in our lives back in 1983 when our income was not sufficient to meet our projected expenses. I got alone with the Lord in a local park, just walking and kicking rocks, telling Him about my problem.

He spoke so clearly and said, "Larry, if you will believe 2 Corinthians 9:8, put it on your lips and in your heart, and if you will speak it out as many times during the day as you can, I will provide for your needs. By the way, please tell me what your budget is." So I told the Lord the minimum that I needed to care for my family. In less than five months our income increased to just what I had told the Lord I needed! However, reflecting on this time in my life, I must admit that for years prior to this time I had been giving sacrificially, even large amounts out of my very need.

Missionary fruit. Fruit for others or ministry. "By this My Father is glorified, that you bear much fruit; so you will be My disciples" (John 15:8). Our work for the Lord will not count for much, unless it is fruit and not the work of our flesh.

All fruit has seed inside of it for reproduction. Genesis 1:11 says, "Then God said, 'Let the land produce vegetation: seed-bearing plants and trees on the land that bear fruit with seed in it, according to their various kinds.' And it was so." Once the interior fruit grows inside of us, it spills out seeds that produce exterior fruit, or ministry to others.

A personal testimony.

I had never really planned to have a ministry such as ISOB. I always had a heart to serve God, however. In 1995 The Lord spoke to me in two ways. He spoke Psalm 68:11, which says, "The Lord gave the word; Great was the company of those who proclaimed it" (Psalms 68:11). He told me that if I wrote and published the Word, that He would see to it that a great host would proclaim it, or re-publish it. He also spoke to me from Mark chapter 14 where it tells the story of a woman who broke her alabaster flask to pour out its costly oil of spikenard on Jesus. The Lord spoke to me and said, "Larry, will you take your substance and pour it out on My Body, just because it feels good to Me?"

These Words or rhemas from the Lord became seeds in my heart, and they are now bearing their fruit! The interesting thing is, that the seeds continually multiply with each piece of fruit, which causes the fruit to grow exponentially! It has and still is, and the nice thing is I really had very little to do with it. Sure I worked hard, but only in obedience to what I heard God speak to my heart. I attempt to avoid "my plans."

How does the seed, or Word, process work?

Mark chapter 4:1-21 tells us the parable of the sower. The entire Kingdom works on this mystery. "He told them, 'The secret of the kingdom of God has been given to you. But to those on the outside everything is said in parables. Without this parable you cannot understand any other parable'" (Mark 4:11).

In this parable Jesus gave us a simple system to use in order to walk in His kingdom with fruitfulness and to be pleasing to Him.

There is no discrimination on race, education, age, sex, intellect, social status or family background. None!

Read Mark 4:1-21. Mark 4:11 says, "He told them, 'The secret of the kingdom of God has been given to you.'" Mark 4:14 says, "The farmer sows the word."

Not only does it work like a seed, but like a mustard seed. Mark 4:30-32 says, "Again he said, 'What shall we say the kingdom of God is like, or what parable shall we use to describe it? It is like a mustard seed, which is the smallest seed you plant in the ground. Yet when planted, it grows and becomes the largest of all garden plants, with such big branches that the birds of the air can perch (abide, live) in its shade.'"

A mustard seed is the smallest seed known. All other vegetable seeds grow into plants, but the mustard seed actually grows into a tree! It is very unusual to have something that looks so insignificant produce something so large! It is also out of character for an herb to become a tree. So it is with the seeds of the Word of God and the Kingdom of God. It does not look like much, but it will provide for all of your needs and for those in your realm of influence, just as the mustard seed does for the birds. Read Luke 17:5 about mustard seed faith.

Every person must choose one of these ways to live their life.

Kingdom of the World	Kingdom of God
Satan is prince.	Jesus is King.
We become his slaves.	We become his slaves.
We use our abilities to meet our needs.	We use His Word to meet our needs-fruit.
We spend our life on things that are worthless in eternity.	We spend our life on things that give us reward in eternity.

But watch out! Satan and his demons are determined to steal your seed. He will not ignore you and allow your seed to grow without a challenge!

There is a process for the fruit to grow. If the process is not followed, the fruit will die. We only have two choices, Grow or Die!

Here is the theme of "Grow or Die." It is God's system for bearing fruit.

1) We need to turn to the Word for fruit.

2) We need to know how to be intimate with God - which is covered in the Flowing River chapter.

3) We need to know how to get out and stay out of being Prisoners in the Promise Land.

4) We need to know more about God's character - Who God is.

5) We need to know our true identity in Jesus - SIT.

6) We need to take up our cross and walk in obedience to the Word - WALK.

7) We need to know about our enemy Satan and how he comes to steal the Word; and how to STAND until victory and fruit comes.

These will be the lessons in the Grow or Die series. They are Scriptural, they work, they are what the Word teaches, and I can testify that God has never failed to use this process in my life.

In John 15:18-27 Jesus warns us that part of the fruit bearing process will be persecution and suffering, but that the Holy Spirit will be there as our comforter.

"Remember the words I spoke to you: 'No servant is greater than his master.' If they persecuted me, they will persecute you also. If they obeyed my teaching, they will obey yours also" (John 15:20). Many people never get their needs met because Satan or his assistants come and steal the Word before it can bear fruit. We need to know that the persecution, trials, and sufferings that we go through do not mean that the fruit is not growing; on the contrary, they are signs that the fruit **is** growing. We need to be wise!

Seeds need nourishment.

They need certain water and minerals. We need to add to the seed sown. There is a process within which a believer in Jesus Christ grows. To understand that process and path, and to cooperate with God in it, will ensure that the believer will Grow. We believe that this Grow or Die course has the water, vitamins and minerals needed for growth.

To be ignorant and/or to refuse to cooperate with God will certainly render the believer a "Prisoner in the Promise Land." The Israelites made it to the Promise Land. In the Book of Judges, the people of God, even though they were in covenant with God, were prisoners to their enemies. Gideon and his people are our examples of prisoners getting free.

In the same way, even today, God's people can be prisoners to fear, guilt, addictions, condemnation, low self-esteem, pride and many other spiritual enemies.

The way to avoid staying in prison is to Grow! The end of the growth process is fruit. Fruit is a result of abiding in the vine that will develop the "missionary" within each believer. Look at the Book of Revelation. The end result after all the battles is fruit, as described in Revelation chapters 20-22.

There are 7 main categories in the Grow or Die process:

Bearing Fruit	(The goal of bearing fruit)
The Flowing River	(Intimacy with God)
Prisoners in the Promise Land	(Our potential condition)
Who God is	(His character)
Sit	(Our position in Christ)
Walk	(Our responsibility)
Stand	(Our victory in warfare)

These are the "seven lead lessons" that make up Section 1 Seminar 1.

Section 2 Seminar 2, consists of 4 additional lessons having to do with The Cross, Demons and Deliverance and Baptism in the Holy Spirit.

Each of the above categories has several individual lessons that may be studied by the student in order to complete the extended course. For the extended course, you will begin with the lessons listed above, and then proceed to the many lessons included in the above main categories. For instance, Who God is has 18 lessons, Sit has 13 lessons, Walk has 41 lessons, and Stand has 11 lessons (there are more in Course 3). You may choose to stop after reading and studying the 11 lessons in this book, or you may continue to complete the course, consisting of over 100 lessons.

It is important for us to know how we learn and how we operate spiritually.

We do not learn spiritual things as we learn secular things, through information processed in our minds. Surely our minds are a part of the process. However, with God we receive revelation, something that is unveiled that was previously veiled to us. Satan puts a veil over our spiritual eyes so that we cannot see (2 Corinthians 4:4). The most important thing to know, however, is that when we receive this revelation, we receive it as a seed, not as fruit. So with each nugget of truth that the Lord reveals to us, we must take it through the process of Who God is, Sit, Walk and Stand. God reveals to us something about Himself, He then applies it to our life (Sit), then we need to obey and Walk it out. For sure, Satan comes to steal the Word, so we must Stand. When we get through this we will bear fruit. See Mark chapter 4 for this Scripture reference.

So this discipleship process is not one big event in our life. No, it is a continual process that we go through, time and time again for each season of our life. It is never ending. We may be standing for one issue and in the sitting process for another issue in our lives.

Following is an outline of the Grow or Die curriculum.

Fruit (This lesson). Trusting the Kingdom of God; the Word of God.

Flowing River. Keeping the branch and the vine connected through fellowship. We need the presence of God in our daily lives. This is a Scriptural and simple map for doing just that in your private devotion time. Ezekiel 47 tells about the River flowing from God's Temple into the lost sea of humanity. We are God's Temple. Intimacy precedes true service!

Prisoners in the Promise Land. Getting free so we are not branches cast into the fire of fruitlessness. Gideon is our example as an Israelite who had a covenant with God living in his God given promise land, yet he was a prisoner to his enemies. What kinds of enemies keep us in bondage? How do we get free?

Who God is. We need constant reminders of Who He is, and that without Him we can do nothing. We will get a quick snapshot of God's character. We will touch on aspects like the Trinity, The Father, Son and Holy Spirit. We will touch on the Word of God, the Virgin Birth and on who God is now.

Sit, Walk, Stand. As a disciple of Jesus Christ it is valuable to know and understand what and how you are learning. There may seem to be so many different things that you feel you need to learn. So often teachings and doctrines will appear to be controversial and in conflict with each other.

For instance, we need to press in to lead a holy life. On the other hand, grace is always there for our failures. So what do we do? Perform and act right, or live any old way and wait for God's grace?

The idea of Sit, Walk, Stand will resolve this apparent conflict. In the book of Ephesians, all three of these issues are addressed. Great credit is given to Watchman Nee and his book, Sit, Walk, and Stand. [1]

SIT: Ephesians 2:6 says, "And God raised us up with Christ and seated us with him in the heavenly realms in Christ Jesus." God wants us to know that Jesus finished all the necessary work for our salvation at the Cross. The finished work of the Cross and the resurrection of Jesus has made a new creation out of us. The old person died, and we were born again. We need to know that God did the work, we did nothing but receive what He accomplished. No matter how many mistakes we may make, forgiveness is there, we are no longer under the law.

Walk: Ephesians 4:1 says, "As a prisoner for the Lord, then, I urge you to live a life worthy of the calling you have received." Now that you know who you are in Jesus, you are asked to become a disciple of Jesus Christ, not a law, but a living person in the form of the Holy Spirit. You are called to walk and live in holiness and righteousness. This is not in any way to earn salvation or favor, but to conform your exterior life to the life of God that is on the inside of you. This is always your choice. A bird must act like a bird, it has no choice, but a Christian may choose to act like a sinner. This is dangerous, because if sin is carried for a long time without confession and repentance, backsliding is imminent. We are not promoting some sort of system of works or legalism. We must always keep in mind that the grace of God is what always takes us to victory.

We are in blood covenant with God now, and a blood covenant requires two deaths. Jesus already did His work, now we are called to do our part.

Luke 9:23-24 says, "Then he said to them all: 'If anyone would come after me, he must deny himself and take up his cross daily and follow me. For whoever wants to save his life will lose it, but whoever loses his life for me will save it.'"

Stand: Our attitude towards the enemy. There is power over the enemy when the two crosses connect. Ephesians 6:10 tells us to Stand against the wiles of the devil as God leads us into his territory. There will be warfare and trouble, but the Holy Spirit will give us comfort. Ephesians 6:11 says, "Put on the full armour of God so that you can take your stand against the devil's schemes." We need to know that there is an active and alive Satan, the devil, who wishes to kill, steal and destroy you and your family. He is very real! He will lie and make you believe that you have no sitting position. He will tempt you to walk the way of the world and your old flesh nature. The devil has been defeated by Jesus, however, he is allowed to lie to us and tempt us. We have some overcoming to do. The victorious Christian life is not easy, our emotions and circumstances tend to lie to us about sitting, walking and standing. But if we stand against the devil, after we know who we are in Jesus, and after we are walking in the Spirit and in repentance, then we can stand until victory comes.

Until we go to heaven we will be involved in a major war with the kingdom of Satan. Victory will come every time if we take sit, walk and stand in their proper place.

"May the peoples praise you, O God; may all the peoples praise you. Then the land will yield its harvest, and God, our God, will bless us" (Psalms 67:5,6).

Chapter 2
The Flowing River

Quote from Watchman Nee from his book <u>A Table in the Wilderness,</u>
June 20. (6)

*"There will I meet with thee, and I will commune with thee from above
the mercy seat, from between the two cherubim which are upon the ark of
the testimony (Exodus 25:22).*

*What is the basis of our communion with God? It is His glory. At the
mercy seat with its shadowing cherubim we have fellowship with God, and
they are "cherubim of glory." It is in the place where God's glory is
manifested, with its implied judgment upon man, that we find mercy there
and there alone. Cannot God, being God, show mercy where he will? No,
he can only show mercy where his moral glory is also maintained. He does
not divorce the mercy seat from the cherubim.*

*It is the shed blood that makes communion possible for sinful man.
Because of it God can show mercy without violating his glory; he can
commune with man without denying himself. Thus the blood of Christ is
essential to fellowship, absolutely essential. Nevertheless it is not the basis
of fellowship. When I commune with blood at his mercy seat it is not on the
precious blood I gaze, but on the glory. The veil is taken away, and with
unveiled face we all behold the glory of God."*

As a child of God you are entitled to experience an ever-deepening
relationship with the Lord. This includes enjoying fellowship in His
presence, but it is much more. Matthew chapter 6 emphasizes reward in
prayer as opposed to answered prayer. The reward is God Himself. Other
results of prayer are simply by-products. If you are sincere about
deepening your relationship with Jesus you may, but there may be a price to
pay. God reveals Himself to those people who submit to and obey Him
(John 14:21). God also reveals Himself to those who seek him diligently
and with pure motives. Often we must remove ourselves from the familiar,
and find time to set aside just for Him. God seems to honor those who
hunger and thirst for true righteousness and holiness. If you do not hunger
for these, at least ask God to give you that hunger.

We know that God's presence never leaves us, but I am talking about
something totally different. I am talking about entering into His glory, His
awesome and very private glory. This is different than corporate worship.
This is just you and God in His Holy of Holies! This kind of encounter
does not necessarily include a manifestation in your physical flesh.
Although it may include that, it may be simply a deep inner and quiet
connection. You experience His glory to such a degree that your life is
eternally transformed. I am talking about a deeper baptism in the Holy
Spirit, beyond the gifts. I am talking about His holiness invading you and
burning off your Adamic nature. As you read on, know that when I use the
word "presence" I am talking about this extra dimensional realm.

When a believer knows with faith that Jesus wants to fellowship with him, he can experience that fellowship provided he submits to God's conditions. His conditions are simply to submit to Jesus as Lord, and to quickly obey His Word. "For all those things My hand has made, And all those things exist, Says the LORD. But on this one will I look (to pay attention to): On him who is poor (afflicted, humble, needy and weak) and of a contrite spirit, And who trembles at My word" (Isaiah 66:2). One major attribute of humility is the wiliness to repent and turn from our old ways, which are unlike God's character.

Those conditions may seem like "old stuff" for many Christians, but there is more to these than may first meet the eye. So many Christians are in "prisons" that are not necessary to be in. They have compromised being real and honest with themselves and with God. They at some point in time knew that they had compromised but now unfortunately they do not even realize that they are in "prison." Often the enemy maintains his prison doors with tactics that are very religious.

Many do not want to face pain, and refuse any type of confrontations. Therefore they compromise not receiving God's best. Others live by rules, legalism, or performance in some sort of pretended holiness. They feel that they are pleasing a harsh God. Still others live by "false grace" feeling that God understands that they are not perfect, therefore why even try to live by faith. They pray when they are in a hard place, but none of these people are enjoying the person of Jesus, the very presence and fellowship of the Creator! They may enter the Kingdom of God when they die, but they are living in Hell while they are on earth.

The Flowing River will build your faith, and will invite God to fulfill His desire to reveal Himself to you. It will also give you some things that you need to do in order to react to His invitation. After I had known the Lord for less than one month I went to a convention and the evangelist made the statement, "The Lord is my best friend. He is closer to me than my wife." When I heard that I became hungry for the same thing, and have pursued it ever since.

Bible studies, sermons, books, discipleship lessons are all good, but if you do not experience the presence of the Lord you are missing the nugget of the Christian life. When you know that Jesus is in the room with you, everything changes. Your joy comes, afflictions seem to diminish, faith rises, and His grace becomes bigger than everything in life that you need to face.

When I discovered this Scriptural path for entering His presence called The Flowing River, my friendship and intimacy with Jesus expanded greatly. I discovered this during times when I could not sense His presence, and when things in life were not going very well with me. I discovered that I could go for a 30-minute walk and in my mind go through the Flowing River pathway, and I would find myself at peace and in contact with the Lord. The goal is to eventually dwell in this place as a lifestyle. This is also a "what to do path" to cooperate with God for getting your practical needs supplied.

People are really hurting.

Some cannot pay their bills, others have received a bad doctor's report, some have children who have gone astray, and perhaps others have families that are falling apart. We need to be able to know how to cooperate with God through the blood covenant lifestyle so that we can make it in this life, between now and the time we leave this body and go to Heaven.

Besides enjoying God's presence, there is a very practical "what to do" path in the Flowing River.

Do we really need to follow a path?

This idea of following a pathway to enter the presence of God is in no way meant to reduce your relationship to God to a formula, or to infer that you must enter into His presence in the way I am going to describe. I do however believe that the Flowing River contains relationship skills that will either enhance your relationship with Jesus or perhaps even allow you to make contact for the very first time.

When my children were very young it was always up to me to initiate relationship times. However as they grew older they began to have more choices and the relationship and fellowship that we could enjoy depended more and more on how they related to me.

The children that would come to me just for friendship, for advice, for appreciation and thanksgiving would always enter into a deeper relationship with me than if they simply came to me for an allowance or to pay a bill. I always had grace, and how they acted never varied my love for them, but I had deeper fellowship with them when they exercised their free wills and their relationship skills. Even if at times they would act in an adverse way my unconditional love would kick in (most of the time). My mercy and grace is what was supposed to draw them to me, but they needed to react and make a choice.

In a sermon recently preached at Southeastern University, Dr. Mark Rutland helped me to put some of this into proper perspective. He said the following:

"We are not trying to access the supernatural, but the supernatural, the Living God, Jesus Himself, is trying to access us. Witchcraft, sorcery, and divination attempts to contact the supernatural."

Response and obedience to God's beckoning is what gives us contact with Him in the supernatural. Again, it is God's initiative that even gives us the desire to obey Him that we might be in contact with His living presence. God is pounding at your door saying, "Please obey Me." Contact with Him often depends upon your obedience.

Obedience is a lifestyle not an event. There is a progressive ladder of obedience. As you live longer the issues for obedience grow and build upon one another. The price continually gets higher. We are called to take up our cross, and we do that. However next time the cross carries a higher price. We never have to take up that old one again, but the new one requires more sacrifice and more obedience because the prize becomes more valuable.

Be prepared! I have seen many people experience Jesus after going through the Flowing River just one time. Make this a habit and your life will change eternally.

God's purpose is to reach a dying world and at the same time bless us. How?

We were blessed in order to become a blessing to a lost and dying world. God told our forefather Abraham, "I will bless those who bless you, And I will curse him who curses you; And in you all the families of the earth shall be blessed" (Genesis 12:3).

The only way we can bless others is to allow Jesus in us to do it through us. The only way He can do it through us is for His character to prevail over our old Adamic nature. This pathway I am going to describe is an opportunity for you to allow God to work His holiness and true righteousness into your life. As you begin to take up your cross and allow the loving God to gently chasten you, you will become more and more like Jesus, a partaker of His character. He will free you from your inner prisons, He will gently bring you to repentance about issues that are hurting you, and your life will never be the same. However, this path is not without pain. If you are lazy, if you will not confront yourself and others who are harming you, you will not enter into this life of fellowship with the Lord. As we become cleansed and become more like Jesus, we enjoy more of His presence, and our lives simply bless others.

Without holiness no man shall see God!

I thank God that righteousness and holiness are legally imputed to us as gifts. But as you deepen your relationship you begin to experience a true and actual transformation of your character into righteousness and holiness. I am not talking about some put on holiness. That kind of religious play-acting produces bitter and angry people, whereas true holiness produces joy, love, and all the fruit of the Spirit. "and that you put on the new man which was created according to God, in true righteousness and holiness" (Ephesians 4:24).

Highway 35. The Highway of Holiness in Isaiah chapter 35.

"A highway shall be there, and a road, And it shall be called the Highway of Holiness. The unclean shall not pass over it, But it shall be for others. Whoever walks the road, although a fool, Shall not go astray" (Isaiah 35:8). Isaiah chapter 33 speaks of the Israelites experiencing judgment due to their sinful lifestyle. Isaiah 34 speaks of God bringing them through the overcoming process and Isaiah chapter 35 shows the result, which is holiness. The benefits are listed in chapter 35. They include joy, singing, the desert and wastelands becoming springs of waters, deserts blooming with roses, abundant rejoicing, seeing the glory of the Lord. It describes blind eyes being opened, feebleness being healed, fear turning into faith, the thirsty given springs of water, and living above your spiritual enemies. It would do you well to study this chapter in this context.

Ezekiel 47:1-12 shows a picture of a flowing river.

The picture God showed to Ezekiel was of the Temple of God, its ordinances and design, and a river flowing from it. God spoke to Ezekiel and showed him that this was a river of life flowing from God down to the Dead Sea into the putrid waters. This river would heal the waters and make them alive. The Scripture in chapter 47 of Ezekiel says that this river started out as a small stream as it came out from under the Temple, but then it progressively became deeper and deeper until it eventually emptied into the Dead Sea. As it did, the Sea became alive with life. The sea in the Bible normally stands for the sea of lost humanity. God was showing Ezekiel that the only way that dead people could live would be to be touched by God through something called a river that was to flow from His very presence. John 7:38 says, "He who believes on Me, as the Scripture has said, 'Out of his belly shall flow rivers of living water.'"

The River flows in to cleanse you – The River flows out to save a dead world

"Write it down Ezekiel."

God told Ezekiel in chapter 43:10-11 to write down this picture of the Temple and its ordinances so that the people could see it and so that they could repent and thus be a blessing to others. That is what this Flowing River lesson is all about.

Where is the temple today? 1 Corinthians 6:19-20 says, "Or do you not know that your body is the temple of the Holy Spirit in you, whom you have of God? And you are not your own, for you are bought with a price. Therefore glorify God in your body and in your spirit, which are God's."

We cannot become blessed nor be a blessing without the real presence of God.

We need the presence of God to set us free and cleanse us in order to do any kind of ministry, even effective prayer. Here is the pattern for experiencing the fullness of the Lord for your life, for your church and for the world. We need the presence of God to set us free and cleanse us in order to do *any* kind of ministry, even effective prayer.

Here is the pattern for experiencing the fullness of the Lord for your life.

"And they were continuing steadfastly in the apostles' doctrine, and in fellowship and in the breaking of the loaves, and in prayers. And fear came on every soul. And many wonders and miracles took place through the apostles" (Acts 2:42-43).

Notice the three things the apostles did daily that resulted in many wonders and miracles:

1. The apostles' doctrine. This is the daily study of the Word of God.

2. Prayers. This most likely included more than one kind of prayer. The early church often confessed who they were in Christ, and confessed the Word.

3. Fellowship and breaking of bread. This was daily communion, or the taking of the cup and the bread in remembrance of the blood covenant.

The early church took communion at least weekly, if not daily. It was their way to enter into the presence of God and experience a deep knowing of Him in a personal way. It was not a religious practice, it was a time of enjoying Him in a real way.

The purpose of communion was to bring the partakers into God's presence. Read Luke 24:30,31 as an example. In it they found healing and all their needs supplied. The presence of God, through His flesh and blood covenant, meets all our needs. (Taken from Dick Reuben's video series, " A Pattern for Revival Fire: Covenant Meal - The Lord's Table.")

The Flowing River is a daily exercise that does the same thing (not to replace communion, but in addition to it). The Flowing River walks one through the blood covenant and brings the person through the veil, which is His flesh, into the Holy of Holies right into His presence! We need His presence daily, not just once in a while!

In John 6:51 Jesus says that He is the Living Bread that came down from Heaven. Hebrews 9:19-20 talks about a new and living way of coming into the Holy of Holies through the veil that is the flesh of Jesus.

What all of this is saying is that the way into the presence of God is through the recognition of the blood covenant; His blood and flesh. You will see that going through the Flowing River recognizes the blood covenant much in the same way as does communion.

We need to know that there are enemies that want to stop God from being real to us.

Our enemies come at us three main ways:
Our will -
Our mind -
Our emotions-
are attacked by Our Flesh, the World and Satan.

Question:
How do we overcome these enemies to get into God's presence for FELLOWSHIP?

Answer:
God has already provided for all victory over all enemies! The way into His presence was provided at the Cross when the veil was torn from top to bottom - Mark 15:38. Now it is our job to cooperate. We must take up our cross - that will give us the victory!

Luke 9:23-25 says, "And he said to them all, 'If any man will come after me, let him deny himself, and take up his cross daily, and follow me. For whosoever will save his life shall lose it: but whosoever will lose his life for my sake, the same shall save it. For what is a man advantaged, if he gain the whole world, and lose himself, or be cast away?'"

The word for *life* in Luke 9 means *"soul"* or the will, mind and emotions. The word *deny* means to say no to.

The key to abundant life and receiving all that Jesus has for us, including His presence, is to complete the blood covenant by taking up our cross.

Many of us know the magnificent, all inclusive, all powerful work done by Jesus on the Cross of Calvary; how He shed his blood for our sin, and rose from the dead to give us life. We cannot add to that. However, in order to take advantage of that work, we must also die. We must take up our cross, deny ourselves and follow Him. We must lose our life.

Our relationship and fellowship with God are based upon a blood covenant. To the Western mindset that can be a foreign thing. The closest comparison we have is marriage, and so many people have an understanding of this relationship that is contrary to the Bible. Ask yourself this: Would you negotiate with your mate-to-be on how many other intimate relationships you are allowed after your marriage?

TWO deaths, Jesus' and yours activate the blood covenant!

What is so important about a blood covenant?

1 Peter 1:18-19 says, "For you know that it was not with perishable things such as silver or gold that you were redeemed from the empty way of life handed down to you from your forefathers, but with the precious blood of Christ, a lamb without blemish or defect."

Leviticus 17:11 says, "For the life of a creature is in the blood, and I have given it to you to make atonement for yourselves on the altar; it is the blood that makes atonement for one's life."

The spiritual life can be exchanged by the law of substitution. A blood covenant changes your family inheritance.

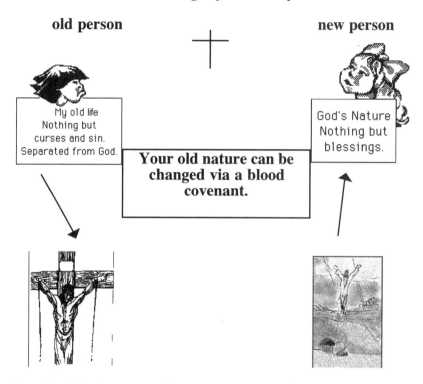

old person   new person

My old life Nothing but curses and sin. Separated from God.

Your old nature can be changed via a blood covenant.

God's Nature Nothing but blessings.

Family inheritance. This basically means that people may be born into a certain family, and from that family lineage they will receive blessings and curses as their inheritance. However blessings and curses can be changed. Tribes in Africa, in American Indian culture and other Asian type societies have always looked for ways to swap or trade blessings and curses with other people.

Since ancient times, people have drank blood that was offered to their god, so that they could be like God.

Before the Foundation of the World, God prearranged to have Jesus crucified according to the *eternal* Spirit, which means that the substitution principle was in effect before any man was created (Revelation 13:8).

In order for a blood covenant to truly be effective, there must be blood shed by two parties, or there must be two deaths and two crosses. We must die to our self and commit all we are and all we have to Jesus. The good thing is that Jesus also commits all He has and all He is to us!

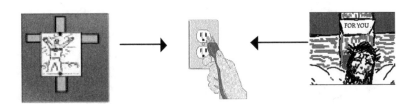

When we connect the Cross of Jesus to our cross we are plugged into God, and Power happens!

There are always two crosses that must connect to make a blood covenant.

The Tabernacle is a powerful symbol of the two crosses to use as a prayer guide. It will help us take up our cross and walk us into the very presence of God for FELLOWSHIP!

"The Old Testament tells us how the chosen people of God lived on earth. At first, the tabernacle served as the center of the 12 tribes; later it was the temple that became their center. The center of the temple was the ark. The tabernacle, the temple and the ark are all types of Christ. As long as the children of Israel maintained their proper relationship with the tabernacle or the temple they were victorious, and no nation could overcome them. Even though their enemies learned how to fight while they themselves were not familiar with fighting, the children of Israel overcame all their enemies nonetheless. But the moment they had problems with the tabernacle or the temple, they were taken into captivity. Nothing else, whether they had powerful kings or great wisdom in themselves mattered at all; the only concern, which mattered, was whether or not they had offended the ark of the tabernacle or temple. If the Lord had the preeminence, then theirs was the victory. So too with us today. In minding the victory of Christ, we also have the victory."

Quote from God's <u>Plan and the Overcomers (6)</u> - Watchman Nee.

As you journey into Fellowship with God, picture taking a walk through the Tabernacle as the priests of the Old Testament did.

The Tabernacle

Outer Court	Holy Place	Holy of
His Cross	Your cross	Holies

Meet with God
in His presence

Bronze Altar
The Cross of
Jesus.

Lampstand
The Mind

The Ark

Mercy Seat
Blood

**Law
Manna
Aaron's Rod**

**Table of
Shewbread**
The Will - Volition

Altar of Incense
Emotions

Presence of
God to meet
with you.

**Brass
Laver** The
Word

Veils

First: His Cross

Under the Old Covenant, Israel held an annual day of atonement, called Yom Kippur. The sins of Israel were to be dealt with on this one day of the year when the high priest prepared to go through the Tabernacle on behalf of Israel for their sins.

At the Bronze Altar, in the outer court, there were two young goats, called calves. One was given a scarlet cloth around its neck indicating it would be slain for blood. The other was tied up outside the gate indicating it was to be the scapegoat. The first goat was slain at the altar and the priest took its blood into the Holy of Holies, where he presented it with incense off the altar of incense (the place of praise). As the incense burned, it filled the Holy of Holies with smoke, which represented (and actually released) the presence of God. The priest would sprinkle the blood on the mercy seat once and in front of it seven times. Outside, every person in the camp lay prostrate through all of this. No one saw any of it happening, yet it meant that his or her sins would be forgiven for the entire year.

Next, as the priest returned and changed his clothes, he laid his hands on the head of the other goat, the scapegoat, symbolizing the transfer of all of the sins to the head of the animal. There was to be a very rugged man chosen to take the scapegoat into the desert wilderness and lead it to a place where it could not return. He would take it to an inescapable place. They would go to a valley surrounded by ledges and cliffs and the goat was lowered down so it could never escape (Leviticus 16:21-22).

Now as the priest laid hands on the scapegoat, beginning the second part of the ceremony, he confessed the sins of the entire Israel. He would say, "Lord, place my sins and the sins of the people on the head of this goat. Now go and depart." As they led the goat out of the camp, all of the people stood and rejoiced. They could all see and understand, even the children. The scapegoat is symbolic of Jesus being our scapegoat, being lowered into Hell for us with our sins on His head. He took our sin and removed it forever, never again to be found or to return. Psalm 103:12 says, "as far as the east is from the west, so has He removed our sin from us." Micah 7:19 says, "that thou will cast all their sins into the depths of the sea."

Hebrews 9:12-14 says, "Neither by the blood of goats and calves, but by his own blood he entered in once into the holy place, having obtained eternal redemption for us. For if the blood of bulls and of goats, and the ashes of an heifer sprinkling the unclean, sanctifieth to the purifying of the flesh: How much more shall the blood of Christ, who through the eternal Spirit offered himself without spot to God, purge your conscience from dead works to serve the living God?"

Second: Our Cross

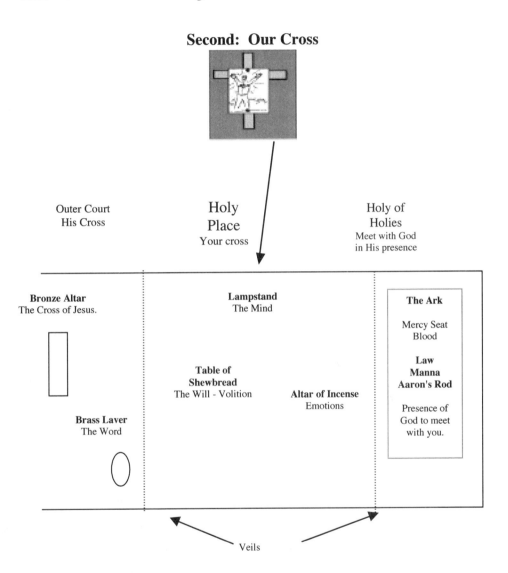

Outer Court His Cross	Holy Place Your cross	Holy of Holies Meet with God in His presence

Bronze Altar
The Cross of Jesus.

Brass Laver
The Word

Lampstand
The Mind

Table of Shewbread
The Will - Volition

Altar of Incense
Emotions

The Ark

Mercy Seat
Blood

Law Manna Aaron's Rod

Presence of God to meet with you.

Veils

When Jesus said that we must deny ourselves, lose our life for His sake, etc., He was using a word that refers to our soul. So we must deny, or say no to, our soul.

Our soul is three parts: will, mind (intellect) and emotions. The Holy Place represents that part of our being, the soul. It has three pieces of furniture that represent our Will, Mind and Emotions (see above picture). Saying no to these and yes to what God has is the taking up of our cross.

Our will -
Our mind -
Our emotions-
are attacked by Our Flesh, the World and Satan.

Now we will take a journey to each of these items in our prayer time and journey right past our enemies into the very presence of God!

Can we really take up our cross without help? We can only take up our cross to a point, but not all the way. We don't have enough hands to crucify all of ourselves; the last nail must be inserted by the world. We must experience some sort of pain and breaking to really get the job done. God does not do this, the world does. We can offer to God those things that we control, those things that we are aware of. However, God sees with vision we do not have. He knows those things in your soul that are keeping you from complete healing and connection with Him. The more of you that can die, the more of Him can live in you. His plan is not to clean up your old life, but to have you experience the crucifixion with Him.

"The Flowing River"
(Daily Prayer Guide)

To Journey Into The Presence of God

Instructions:

1. Read the first 7 pages first, then again at least once a month. Then start here on this page on a daily basis, taking at least twenty minutes to make contact with God.

2. When you start through the tabernacle your back is to be toward the world and your face toward Jesus. This is important, for the Holy Spirit will not honor you with His presence if you are facing in the wrong direction (spiritual direction, Acts 26:18).

3. Go to each "stop" and deal with that subject in prayer with the Lord. Look up some of the Scriptures. Be alert for areas of repentance, for this is one of our main contributions toward this fellowship time with God.

4. It is preferred that you go through all these stops at one time. You can do it in *twenty minutes*. However, if you do not have time in one sitting to go through this entire process, do not give up. Instead, begin the process in the morning, and go through at least one step. Then, do the next one at lunch. If you need to, go ahead and continue the next day. Eventually, live a life of this process and it will be a natural process of always staying in His presence.

The Outer Court

First Stop: **The Bronze Altar - The Cross of Jesus.**

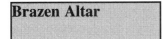

Forgiveness.

The blood covenant swaps everything that we have that is bad for everything that God has that is good. However, we cannot have forgiveness of sins without making Jesus Lord (Romans 10:9-10).

Start out today by being honest with Jesus. 1 John 1:9 says, "If we confess our sins He is faithful and just to forgive us our sins and cleanse us from all unrighteousness."

A big part of taking up your cross is being GUT LEVEL HONEST with God. You need to be totally transparent and tell Him everything. Take time to pour out your heart to him as you would your best friend! 1 John 1:7 says, "But if we walk in the light, as He is in the light, we have fellowship with one another, and the blood of Jesus Christ His Son cleanses us from all sin." Jesus said in John 3:19 that sin had no power as long as people came out into the light with the truth, and did not attempt to hide in darkness. Jesus did not die for our excuses; He died for our sin!

Here are some relationship disciplines that we feel are extremely important if you are going to pursue an authentic relationship with the Lord Jesus.
Relationship Disciplines and Skills.
God is inviting you to discipline your life to relate to Him and get to know Him. This is how the blood covenant blessings flow into your life:
1. Make a firm decision to pursue the relationship. Offer yourself completely to God (Romans 12:1-2). This is our blood covenant response to a mighty blood covenant offered to us by God.
2. Take time to listen. You must take in His Word. Words are blood covenant containers. You must always be in a disciplined Bible study of some kind. Ask the Holy Spirit to show you.
3. Take time to talk. Speak your words. Some people write down your thoughts and feelings in a journal, which can be very valuable. If you have never taken time to be honest with God, you should write down your thoughts, emotions and feelings daily in a journal. You will see God speak back to you! Be gut level honest. Honesty with your blood covenant partner Jesus will cause your sin to go on Him. You cannot and will not overcome any bondage without this gut level honesty.
4. Take time to talk. Speak His Words. Read Psalms and Proverbs by the day. One discipline is to read aloud five Psalms every morning. Use the system of the calendar. As an example, on the 24th of the month read Psalms 24, 54, 84, 114 and 144. Also read Proverb 24. In this system the student will read all Psalms and Proverbs every month. Using this system renews the mind, speaks the Word to Satan, and allows the suffering believer to relate his/her emotions to the Psalmist's. Provisions can be made for months with 31 days, and for Psalm 119. God may lead you to other Scriptures to read out loud as you progress, but this is a good start, and can be a continued blessing for the rest of your life.
5. Obey God. Ask God to give you something simple, something small every day that you may obey. It may be just encouraging another. It may be not driving down the same street that fed your addiction. It may be confessing your sin to Him.
This is a big thing!
John 14:21-23 says that when we obey His Word that He will reveal more and more of Himself to us. Once you have "seen" Jesus, your relationship with Him will no longer be a discipline, but it will be a passionate pursuit. The apostle Paul had this passion when he said in Philippians 3:10, "[For my determined purpose is] that I may know Him [that I may progressively become more deeply and intimately acquainted with Him, perceiving and recognizing and understanding the wonders of His

Person more strongly and more clearly], and that I may in that same way come to know the power outflowing from His resurrection [which it exerts over believers], and that I may so share His sufferings as to be continually transformed [in spirit into His likeness even] to His death, [in the hope]."

6. Communion. Take communion on a regular basis. Many people take it daily.

7. Stay in fellowship. It is important to be in fellowship with strong Bible believing, Spirit filled believers, for refreshing and encouragement.

You need to walk in love, and when you fail, run to God to be cleansed.

"The Law of the Spirit of Life in Christ Jesus has set us free from the Law of Sin and Death"(Romans 8:2). If we stay turned toward God and stay honest with Him, He will see us through even in our mistakes and stumbling.

Look at the Flowing River Appendix F and give yourself an honest evaluation.

If there are no known sins then confess Galatians 2:20 and 2 Corinthians 5:21.

Second Stop: The Laver: The Word of God

Brass Laver

Now that our conscience is clear and we can make contact with God, let's get into the Word.

The Word says that the priest would die if he tried to get into the Holy Place without stopping at the Laver. We cannot proceed into God's presence without being cleansed by the Word of God (Ephesians 5:26-27).

The Laver will cleanse us from the filth of the world. It will also be a mirror to judge us; it will bring things to our mind that we need to get right with God. The Word will renew our mind so that we can think spiritually and stand against the words that demons speak into our minds.

The Word also tells us that Satan is judged (John 16:11). Be sure to say this out loud " Satan you have been judged a loser!"

Spend a few minutes in the Word!

   a. Use your devotion book.

   b. Use your ISOB or other Bible study book.

   c. Read the Proverb for today.

   d. Read one or more Psalms.

   e. Read other books about the Bible, or just read the Bible and ask The Holy Spirit to interpret. Read through the Bible in a year's time.

   f. Listen to some teaching or music tapes that have the Word.

Third Stop: The First Veil:

First Veil: Thanksgiving

Come into His gates with Thanksgiving, into His courts with Praise.

Now that you have been in the Word, you know you are right with God, Satan is judged. You have a lot to be thankful for! Even if you do not have things around you to be thankful for, try to find some. Thank Him that you are saved and going to Heaven.

Just thank Him for what the Word says. Thank Him because the Word says to and because you know you have victory if you hang on. Thank Him for the promises that He made to you that have not come into your life as yet. Thank Him because you know that He wants to take all of unfavorable circumstances in your life and turn them into something beautiful. Thanking Him is a major relationship skill. Children always stay in better relationship with their parents when they are grateful as opposed to always begging and complaining.

Fourth Stop: Your Will

Table of Shewbread The next Stop is inside the Holy Place. This is where you give Jesus your will for His will, your mind for His mind, your emotions for His emotions. This is taking up your cross, denying yourself and following Jesus (Luke 9:23). Only you can tell God to take all of your heart, He will not violate your will. He needs to hear you tell Him about the things of your will that you are surrendering to Him.

Exchange the desires of your heart (even if they may be good) for God's plan or will for your life. Lay down your wants, desires and plans and ask God for His.

God is continually looking at our will; that is what Shewbread means. Bread is ground up flour, mixed with oil and baked in the fire. Our will and our desires must be continually offered up to the altar to be ground and burned. This is a very special sacrifice to God, for it is *our* will, and He will not overwhelm, nor control us. Offer your body a living sacrifice, so that we may prove that perfect will of God (Romans 12:1-2).

Make up your mind to forgive even if you do not feel like it.

This is an opportunity to repent, to turn from the paths and ways of the world toward God's paths. When we turn, we get the power of God (Acts 26:18 and II Cor. 3:16).

Exchange the lusts of the flesh for the fruit of the Spirit. The fruit of the Spirit: love, joy, peace, patience, kindness, goodness, faithfulness, gentleness and self-control (Galatians 5:19-23).

Fifth Stop: Your mind

Golden Lampstand

Exchange your old thoughts for the mind of Christ. 2 Corinthians 10:4-6 tells us the warfare is in our mind. It tells us that strongholds are our reasonings that holds captive our thoughts, and these thoughts keep us from the true knowledge of God. There is much to be said here because our thoughts are the very core of our being. We must set our thoughts free! How? When we were slaves to sin, we used the Tree of Knowledge of Good and Evil, which is our reasoning. Now we should be using the Tree of Life, which is the Word of God. I no longer think and decide, but I use my mind for it's God given purpose, and that is to listen and obey! This alone will destroy the strongholds in our minds. When we truly see the Glory of God as Paul did on the road to Damascus, we no longer reason, we simply say, "Lord what do you desire for me to do." Take your negative thoughts captive by bringing them honestly to the Cross; giving them to Jesus as something you do not want. This is powerful!

Demons constantly accuse us and bombard our minds with half-truths. Isaiah 11 tells us that God replaces our natural intellect with that of the Holy Spirit: i.e., Spirit of The Lord, knowledge, counsel, wisdom, understanding, might and fear of the Lord.

We need to get our mind renewed by the Holy Spirit and the Word of God (Romans 12:2). Sometimes our intellect does not know how to pray. Romans 8:26 says we should use our prayer language to pray God's perfect will. Every time you use your prayer language, you are praying out God's Word and God's will. Your speech center dominates the entire brain, so your mind is being renewed and smoothed out to tell your flesh to conform to God's will.

The Helmet of Salvation. Our brain needs salvation from cleverness, from allowing our mind and intellect to take God's place in our lives. Without this, we will never walk in God's perfect will for our lives (Romans 12:1-2). More often than not, this is not something that we can or will voluntarily give up. Usually it takes a "breaking," a set of circumstances that take us beyond what our brain can negotiate and/or solve. Only then can we quietly wait on God for Him to speak and be silent while He works out our lives.

The Lampstand traditionally represents testimony. We should utilize our intellectual powers to speak God's Word as a testimony to the enemy.

Sixth Stop: Your Emotions

Altar of Incense

Exchange your old emotions induced by your flesh and the World, for God's fruit of peace, joy, love, hope, etc.

This is the place of a sacrifice of praise. Read Psalms 145-150 out loud if you do not *feel* the praise in your heart. God is seeking those who worship Him in Spirit and in Truth (John 4:24). From this point of praise, God will seek you and desire your company!

Give Him those emotions that you have been holding back; perhaps your tears, maybe the raising of your hands, or perhaps just revealing to Him your true emotions. Go ahead, no one is looking except Him!

In front of this altar is the thick veil that hides the Holy of Holies and the presence of God. God wants you to come through the veil more than you desire to. He will pull you through. No natural man could go here without dying.

This veil tore from top to bottom when Jesus died on the Cross, giving us entry into God's presence by His blood and indicating that His death removed the obstacle that sin created for coming into the very presence of God. Praise Him for this fact.

The Holy of Holies is the place where there is no light except for God. The High Priest could only go here once a year, and only under certain conditions. The incense censor from this altar actually went into the Holy of Holies with the High Priest once a year. This symbolizes that your praise and worship do not stop here but that they are the entry into His presence, and they go with us.

Your destination: Now God pulls you through the veil into the Holy of Holies -The very presence of God.

Your Spirit - God's presence

Ark of the Covenant

Here is the Ark of The Covenant. It is covered by the Mercy Seat that is sprinkled with blood. We needed mercy at the Bronze Altar, the Cross, in the very beginning. However, now in His presence is a new dimension of realizing His mercy and the blood of Jesus in a way that only the Holy Spirit can show you. His mercy endures forever. It is almost impossible to write about, it must be experienced. This is when the seed of the Word is planting in your heart. When the Word of God is anointed by the presence of the Holy Spirit, it is powerful!

On either side are huge angels protecting everything. There is no light in here at all except for the Light of God.

Remember, the Ark of The Covenant is now in our heart! It is no longer an external thing. We are the Temple of God. Meditate on that. "Don't you know that you yourselves are God's temple and that God's Spirit lives in you?" (1 Corinthians 3:16).

The Ark contents symbolize three main things:

The manna, or the Word of God: When you are in God's presence, the revealed Word of God comes alive! The Bible becomes Scriptures, the Scriptures become the Word, and the Word becomes flesh. The Word is now in you! If you have time, this is a great place to open your Bible and let the Lord speak. Manna also speaks of our provisions. All of our provisions, love, security and significance are already inside of us. This includes everything we need for life and godliness. Fruit for our provisions here on earth is provided by God's Word (2 Peter 2:1-11).

Tablets of Law: This is a precious reminder that the Law of God is written on our hearts. It is no longer a list of do's and don'ts.

Aaron's Rod: This signifies our anointed ministry to be workers and prayer warriors for God. There were 12 broken almond rods placed in the Temple at God's command. The one that would supernaturally bud during the night, would be the one whose owner would be God's appointed minister. Only God has our ministry for us, and we only realize what it is when we are in His presence (Numbers 17:8).

Here is where we can really receive the promises of God in His Word. When we receive them here, we know that we will have them! Philippians 4:19 says, "My God will supply your every need according to His riches in Glory in Christ Jesus." Here you are in Glory! Here are all the riches of Heaven waiting for you.

Begin to thank God that these three things are not just in front of you, but they are *in* you. Not only are they *in* you, but also the blood and mercy seat and angels are protecting you with them. Psalm 91 says that the angels protect you in your way of service and obedience.

Now you are equipped to be a real intercessor. You are sharing in the High Priestly ministry of Jesus and praying for others effectively. Jesus said in John 15: 7, "If you abide in Me, and My words abide in you, you shall ask what you will, and it shall be done to you."

This would be a great time to just sit back and bask in the presence of God. Take some time here to be quiet and enjoy being with Him. You do not even have to talk. God enjoys this, and you will too. This is what this lesson is all about, coming into the presence of God! Do not just read this and go on.

Determine that you will practice the presence of God on a daily basis. It is the main ingredient for victory in this life and the next.

Appendix F
A Spiritual Check-up.

- **Love** - Are you treating others with the unconditional love of God?
- **Selfishness** - Putting your own needs over the needs of others. Love is concerned with the welfare of the other person; are you more concerned with yourself and how you feel?
- **Stealing** - Can you remember taking money for property that was not yours?
- **Cheating** - Did you get anything from anyone unfairly?
- **Lying** - Any designed form of deception.
- **Slander** - Speaking evil of someone. You do not have to lie to slander. Have you spoken about others without love?
- **Immorality** - Are you guilty of stirring up desires that you could not righteously feed? Sexual vice, all impurity, even against your own body.
- **Drunkenness**, drugs sorcery, carousing.
- **Foul or polluted language**, evil words, unwholesome or worthless talk. Filthiness, foolish, silly, and corrupt talk.
- **Envy** - Behind the talk of other's failures and faults usually lurks envy.
- **Ingratitude** - How many times have others done things for you that you are not grateful for?
- **Anger** - Have you been bad-tempered?
- **Cursing** - Have you used gutter language?
- **Needless silly talk.** Talking and acting like a moron. Jests and practical jokes that tend to undermine the sacred and precious standards of life. Have you made fun of an ethnic group or a certain part of the world, a state or region in your country, or some politician? Ethnic and regional jokes have no place in holiness.
- **Hardness** - Did you fight back, murmur or return evil for evil?
- **Habits** - Have you continually over-indulged natural appetites; how about your eating habits?
- **Halfhearteness** - Can you remember times when you deliberately shirked your full share of responsibility?
- **Hindrance** - Have you destroyed another's confidence in you by needlessly taking up their time? Have you betrayed another's confidence in you?
- **Hypocrisy** - Did the life you lived before some people make all you said of Christ and His gospel a lie?
- **Broken Vows** - Is there a vow you made to God that you have not kept?
- **Unforgiveness** - Are you holding any resentment against anyone, friend or foe?
- **Divisions**, clicks, the party spirit of having differing groups.
- **Lustful,** rich and wasteful living, greediness. Overspending on shopping, Wasting time.

- **Not treating** wives, husbands, children, and parents with love and honor.
- **Not being content**, being jealous of what others have and you do not have.
- **Love of money -** A person without any money can still have the love of money.
- **Idolatry -** Any desire in your life above your desire for God.
- **Strife** - Have you stirred up strife by unneeded words?
- **Witchcraft** - Manipulating another to meet your needs.
- **Rebellion to authority** - Boss, teacher, parent, spiritual leader, etc.
- **Love of the World** - Includes: Sins of the eyes - What are you reading or watching? Lust of the flesh - What are you desiring? Pride of life - What part of your life do you think you can handle without God being involved? - Pretending in thought or life to be more or less than you really ARE.
- **Pride** is the greatest sin of all. Examine these areas:
- Do you focus on the failure of others or are you concerned with your own sense of spiritual need?
- Are you self-righteous and critical or compassionate and forgiving, looking for the best in others?
- Do you look down on others or esteem all others better than yourself?
- Are you independent and self-sufficient or dependent, recognizing your need for others?
- Must you maintain control or do you surrender control?
- Do you have to prove you are correct, or are you willing to yield the right to be correct?
- Do you have a demanding spirit or a giving spirit?
- Do you desire to be served or are you motivated to serve others?
- Do you desire to be promoted or are you happy when others are promoted?
- Do you need to receive the credit or are you happy when others are recognized?
- Do you feel confident in how much you know or are you humbled by how much you have yet to learn?
- Are you self-conscious or not concerned with yourself at all?
- Do you keep people at arm's length or do you risk getting close to others. Are you willing to take the risk of loving intimately?
- Are you quick to blame others or do you accept responsibility?
- Are you unapproachable or easy to be entreated?
- Are you defensive when criticized or receive criticism with a humble and open heart?
- Are you concerned with being respected or being real?
- Are you concerned about what others think or what God thinks?

- Do you work to maintain your image or do you die to your reputation?
- Do you find it difficult to share your spiritual needs with others or are you willing to be open and transparent?
- Do you try to hide your sin or are you willing to be exposed when you are wrong?
- Do you have a hard time saying, "I was wrong, will you please forgive me?"
- When confessing sin, do you deal in generalities or do you deal in specifics?
- Are you remorseful over your sin when you get caught or are you grieved over your sin and quick to repent?
- When there is a misunderstanding or conflict, do you wait for others to come and ask forgiveness or do you take the initiative?
- Do you compare yourself with others and feel deserving of honor or do you compare yourself to the holiness of God and feel a desperate need for mercy?
- Do you think you have little or nothing to repent for or do you have a continual attitude of repentance.
- Do you think that everyone else needs revival or do you continually sense a need for a fresh encounter with the filling of the Holy Spirit?
- Are you proud when you are around a new Christian or do you delight in his/her zeal? Are you willing to learn from him/her?
- Are you intimidated when you are around a more mature Christian, or are you hungry to learn from his/her experience?

Surgery needed?

If the Holy Spirit shows us sin, we must go back to the place where the Lord first met us. It is the Cross again. We see the Lord Jesus once crucified for that sin, bearing our penalty.

A line of blood trickles down from The Cross' splintered base. The sight should shock and grieve us because we see the awfulness of God's judgment. We need to understand that all of God's wrath and judgment was put on Jesus at the Cross.

Jesus is waiting there for us, not to condemn us, but happy to have us come to the Cross to give Him our sin. So many Christians run from God in shame and guilt when they discover sin. Past sins, mistakes and bad decisions, if left unchecked, will block God's presence from you.

God wants you to grow up and learn and not make the same mistakes again, however bringing you into His presence without shame and guilt is extremely important to Him. That is the only way you can glorify God and be free from all bondages. Romans 8:1-2 says that there is indeed the Law of Sin and death. What you sow is what you will reap. The law of sowing and reaping is absolute for the good seed, however for the bad seed there is a remedy. That remedy is the Law of the Spirit of Life, which nullifies the Law of Sin and Death.

"There is therefore now no condemnation to those who are in Christ Jesus, who do not walk according to the flesh, but according to the Spirit. For the law of the Spirit of life in Christ Jesus has made me free from the law of sin and death. For what the law could not do in that it was weak through the flesh, God did by sending His own Son in the likeness of sinful flesh, on account of sin: He condemned sin in the flesh, that the righteous requirement of the law might be fulfilled in us who do not walk according to the flesh but according to the Spirit" (Romans 8:1-4).

God's remedy for sin is to come to the Cross, come to the Holy of Holies into His presence and let His character flood your character. His holiness will replace your sin. This is the only remedy. We cannot do it ourselves. It is the displacement method. We do not empty out our sin, God floods us with His holiness and love and the sin must leave. Do not be discouraged if you have to do this time and time again. God is not the one who condemns, Satan is. God will take you back as many times as you come. When you stop coming is when He is grieved.

Walk out into the light of reality. Drop your self-deceit and face this sin for what it really is. Turn from it, from your heart. Take sides with God against it. Purpose in your heart NEVER to go back into that sin again.

Confession:

"If we confess our sins, He is faithful and just to forgive us our sins, and to cleanse us from all unrighteousness"(I John. 1:9).

"The LORD is compassionate and gracious, slow to anger, abounding in love. He will not always accuse, nor will he harbour his anger for ever; he does not treat us as our sins deserve or repay us according to our iniquities. For as high as the heavens are above the earth, so great is his love for those who fear him; as far as the east is from the west, so far has he removed our transgressions from us" (Psalms 103:8-12).

Forgiveness is not excusing. Forgiveness is a strong word that means to cut away and remove like a surgeon cuts out a cancer. Forgiveness of sin means that the sin is removed from you and put on to Jesus who bore it on the Cross.

Confession is agreeing with how God sees the matter and speaking it with your mouth. Confession is not just saying it, confession includes being in agreement with the Word. Humility is admitting you are wrong.

Will you do this now? Will you go to your gracious and loving Father as a little child and humbly ask His forgiveness and confess your sin?

"Oh God, You know my foolishness, and my sin is not hid from You...for Your Name's sake, pardon my iniquity, for it is great...If you, Lord, would mark iniquities, who shall stand? But there is forgiveness with You, that You may be feared.

Oh God, my Father, I come to you to confess my sin(s) of: (Now list and confess them.)

Your Word says that these acts and/or these attitudes are sin, and I hereby agree with Your Word. I call this sin what it is. I make no excuses for it. I no longer want to hold this sin in my spirit, soul and body. I want to get it out and expel it. It is separating me from You. It is destroying me. I want to be healed, spirit, soul and body, and I want to be close to you. I accept your forgiveness. Thank you for putting this sin on Jesus, and thank you that He took it to His Cross for me. I know I do not deserve this exchange, but I am so thankful to be free."

Restitution is the willingness to pay back or restore wherever possible. If you are now forgiven before the Lord, are you ready to ask Him for the courage to confess and restore to others you have wronged? Your conscience must be clean before both God AND man if you want to know true freedom. You cannot stand for God with a dirty past in other's eyes.

Memories of your failure in their eyes will drive you deeper into bondage each time you remember them. If you have not asked their forgiveness, your guilt will kill your faith and rob you of direction and purpose. You will not, of course, have to confess every sin to everyone; just the sins committed against the ones you know you have wronged.

The rule: The circle of confession should only go as far as the circle of committal. Those sins against God alone, you have left with His loving forgetfulness (Ps. 103:8-13; Is. 43:25; Jer. 31:34). Those against God and man must be made right with BOTH God and the person(s) wronged.

Portions of this Appendix F were taken from Winkie Pratney's tracts published on the World Wide Web.

Chapter 3
Prisoners in the Promise Land

The Old Testament was given as a type and warning to us to learn from.

1 Corinthians 10:11 says, "These things happened to them as examples and were written down as warnings for us, on whom the fulfillment of the ages has come."

The Promise Land in the Old Testament was the land of Canaan. It was not a place that was perfect, but a place where Israel's enemies dwelt; a place of war and struggle. Our Promise Land is not Heaven, it is the here and now, inheriting God's promises in our lives as Christians. Our enemies are still here and can still take us prisoners, even in our promise land! Just because we are Christians we are not immune from Satan's prisons.

In the Old Testament the Israelites were prisoners in their Promise Land. Christians can be, and are, prisoners to Satan and they do not know it. We can have strongholds that keep us from fulfilling our God given purpose in life. A stronghold is a mindset that accepts as inevitable or unchangeable, something hat is contrary to the revealed will of God. [1]

Satan could no longer hold God's people in famine, so he tried to hold them in Egyptian slavery. He tried, again, to wipe them out in the desert on their way to the Promise Land, but he could not stop them at the Jordon River, nor at Jericho. But when they got into the Promise Land, he got them at a little town called Ai. Why? Because of their own sin. It was an internal enemy, not a visible military power (Joshua 7).

The Israelites were still prisoners after they had reached their promise land!

"Then the children of Israel did evil in the sight of the LORD. So the LORD delivered them into the hand of Midian for seven years, and the hand of Midian prevailed against Israel. Because of the Midianites, the children of Israel made for themselves the dens, the caves, and the strongholds [2] which *are* in the mountains. So it was, whenever Israel had sown, Midianites would come up; also Amalekites and the people of the East would come up against them. Then they would encamp against them and destroy the produce of the earth as far as Gaza, and leave no sustenance for Israel, neither sheep nor ox nor donkey. For they would come up with their livestock and their tents, coming in as numerous as locusts; both they and their camels were without number; and they would enter the land to destroy it. So Israel was greatly impoverished because of the Midianites, and the children of Israel cried out to the LORD" (Judges 6:1-6).

---

[1] "For the weapons of our warfare *are* not carnal but mighty in God for pulling down strongholds, casting down arguments and every high thing that exalts itself against the knowledge of God, bringing every thought into captivity to the obedience of Christ" (2 Corinthians 10:4).

For hundreds of years, the Israelites called out to God and He delivered them in their pain. Then they got into idolatry again and became prisoners to something else. Why?

"And I said to you, I am the LORD your God. Do not fear the gods of the Amorites in whose land you live. *But you have not obeyed My voice (Word)" (Judges 6:10).*

In Judges 6 God came to Gideon in his situation. The Hebrews were in their Promise Land, but every time they planted seed, the Midianites and the Amalekites would raid the area and stomp out the crops. They would steal the seed just as Satan steals the seed of the Word of God. So these children of God were actually prisoners to their enemy, even though they were in the Promise Land.

The Old Testament shows God's people living as prisoners in the promise land.

Ha, even if they are Christians I can still take them captive!

This is how the enemy works to trap you.

He looks for those works of your flesh (your old nature) that you will not forsake. He convinces you that you do not need to live on the Word of God, but that you can make it for yourself. He convinces you that you do not need to use God's Kingdom and His system of bearing fruit. Unforgiveness is a major invitation for the devil to operate in your life.

After a while he latches on to those works and you become deceived by this demon. You are not demon possessed, but you are demon influenced. These become strongholds and you feel hopeless. You are a Christian in God's promise land, but you are a prisoner like the people in the Old Testament. You are no longer a candidate for waters to flow out of you to help others. Satan has stopped up the River, but you have given him permission.

What are some Prisons that Satan can keep us in?
"Jesus answered them, Truly, truly, I say to you, Whoever practices sin is the slave of sin" (John 8:34).
Sickness, disease.
Continual lack of finances.

Being unloved. If we have not received unconditional love from our parents, we are in a prison.

Selfishness, or self-love is the opposite of real love. This is thinking that you are the center of the world and all things revolve around you.

Low self-esteem - a sense of unworthiness and defeat. We are not to receive our sense of who we are from anywhere or anyone except God and His Word. Human nature and the world attempts to paste a false sense of who we are onto us. Either we feel we are superior and prideful, or we feel unworthy with shame and inferiority. A good way to battle this is to know that God lives inside of you, and everywhere you go is blessed because you are carrying God with you. You bless everyone you meet because you are a clay vessel filled with the glory of God. What others think of you does not make you who you are. Your job or vocation does not identify you. When you go to your job, you are giving it dignity. When Jesus washed the feet of His disciples, it was like cleaning toilets, but because God was doing it, washing feet has become an honorable thing.

Widows and Orphans. James 1:27. God puts special emphasis on the plight of widows (this definition includes divorced women) and orphans (this definition includes children of divorce). It has to do with having no authority, no covering, and no fathering figure. It involves being left without defense, without an advocate in the ultimate sense. The Old Testament is full of warnings to Israel to take care of the fatherless and to care for the widows. It should be no less for the Church today.

We all need security, and being either a widow or an orphan is the ultimate in the lack of security. I know people who have had a difficult time recovering from becoming a widow or an orphan. As believers, we are to represent the heart of God towards widows and orphans. His heart is to look out for them, to give them special comfort and to provide for them. He is their covering, He is their security. If you have been this type of a "prisoner," you need to know that God says in James 1:27 that true worship, true "religion" and the fear of God involves showing His heart of love and care towards widows and orphans. This is a very serious statement by God, and you need to know how much He is interested in and cares for you!

"In His holy dwelling God *is* the father of the fatherless, and the judge of the widows" (Psalms 68:5).

Mammon - trusting in the world, other people, or anything else for your material needs, rather than God.

Abuse - So many people have been abused, sexually and in other ways.

Self-righteousness is a very big one.

Unforgiveness is a major one.

Other enemies are guilt, moral sins, sexual sin, bitterness, gossip, anger, compromising integrity and truth, and the list goes on.

Addictions - There are too many to name, but they are a substitute for God's love through the Holy Spirit.

Many are trapped in generational curses such as the inability to express love and kindness, the slavery mindset, being a people pleaser, being a perfectionist or performance oriented for self-esteem. Many of these areas manifest themselves in broken or compromised relationships, the inability to live in peace, the inability to be content.

Witchcraft or the control of others. You may be the victim or the perpetrator.

Guilt and shame from your past. Jesus gives us a fresh start and wipes away our past.

However, I believe that one of the most widespread issues is rejection.

I believe that rejection is the root of hundreds of other problems. We need the unconditional acceptance from our parents when we are young. Broken relationships with our fathers is a widespread cause of bondages to drugs and other addictions.

We need acceptance from our peers, our spouses, etc. In today's society, broken people inflict damage on others through rejection and it spreads from generation to generation. We are not able to pass love on without having first received it. 1 John 4:19 says, "We love because he first loved us." God's remedy for rejection is two fold:

1) He took our rejection and bore it for us. Isaiah 53:3, says, "He was despised and rejected by men, a man of sorrows, and familiar with suffering. Like one from whom men hide their faces he was despised, and we esteemed him not."

2) He accepts us unconditionally with His great love! Ephesians 1:6, says, "To the praise of the glory of his grace, wherein he hath made us accepted in the beloved."

Jesus is not condemning us for these areas. Jesus wants to set us free. This is His mission. But we need to be honest with ourselves, drop our pride, and be prepared to cooperate with the healing process of getting free.

Notice what was the bottom line and root cause of the bondage of these people.

"And I said to you, I am the LORD your God. Do not fear the gods of the Amorites in whose land you live. *But you have not obeyed My voice (Word)" (Judges 6:10).*

Gideon is our example of a prisoner that became free and even freed his people!

Gideon bore fruit for God. He was working hard at making life work with his own power, but he ended up with failure, low self-esteem and hopelessness. He was hiding in his wine vat underground in order to avoid the Midianites who would come in hordes and wipe out the crops and steal the livestock. No matter how hard he and his people tried, they could not overcome the enemy. The Midianites were those enemies that beat down God's pastures and robbed the seed. In the same way today's Midianites, demons, rob the Word of God to keep us from being fruitful. Notice that they waited until Israel had sown their crops, then they swarmed down to destroy them. They came as grasshoppers. Israel was greatly impoverished.

What did God do? What did Gideon do?

The primary lesson that I want us to learn is that God taught Gideon to hear His voice!

Watch and see how the relationship between God and Gideon developed from glory to glory. See how Gideon cooperated with God's leading, and how God provided the grace and the power. Gideon learned to obey His voice. That is really all he had to do. That is really any of us need to do. Notice, God did not say, "You have not obeyed My laws or My precepts or principles." He said, "You have not obeyed My voice." One's voice is personal compared to laws, commands and precepts. Voice is personal it is face to face. It is powerful to hear God's voice. It really does not matter what He says, just as long as His voice can be heard.

The question is: How desperate are you to hear God's voice? How desperate are you to obey His voice.

The end of the story is that Gideon was used by God to motivate a victory and freedom for people, not just for himself. As Isaiah 61 shows, he went from prisoner to priest. He went from a sufferer to a comforter. He turned his junk into jewels. He took the path of the cross to the grave to the resurrection.

In this study we are going to see how God worked, and still works to turn our prisons into freedom. We will also see how Gideon responded to God so that we may follow his steps for our own lives.

Follow Gideon's path in Judges chapter 6.

6:1 He was a victim of his forefather's idol worship. His people were in bondage to poverty due to the past 200 years of idol worship. The first thing we need to do is to forgive those that put us into these prisons. Without this forgiveness, as an act of our will, the rest of the process will not work. If we cannot find forgiveness, then confess that as sin to the Lord and His forgiveness will work through us.

6:1-11 He was hiding in his wine vat underground in order to avoid the Midianites who would come in hordes and wipe out the crops and steal the livestock. No matter how hard he and his people tried, they could not overcome the enemy. The Midianites were those enemies that beat down God's pastures and robbed the seed.

In the same way today's Midianites, demons, rob the Word of God to keep us from being fruitful. Notice that they waited until Israel had sown their crops, and then they swarmed down to destroy them. They came as grasshoppers. Israel was greatly impoverished.

6:8 God spoke to the Israelites. In God's mercy, He heard the cries of the Israelites and sent a prophet. His mercy endures forever. The prophet told the Israelites that God was their God, He had delivered them from bondage once and that the reason they were in bondage again (this time in their own Promise Land) was that they did not obey the voice of God (The Word of God). If we do not LIVE on the Word of God daily, we will surely become slaves and prisoners to our enemies. There is no way around it.

6:12 God spoke to Gideon personally. The angel of the Lord, the personal representative of God, came to Gideon. The Amplified Bible commentary says that this was an Old Testament appearance of Jesus. He called Gideon a "Mighty Man of Valor." Why did He use these words to someone who was acting like a coward, who had no self-esteem and was threshing wheat in hiding so that his enemies could not spot him? God always deals with us this way; He sees what we will become. He calls those things that are not as though they are (Romans 4:17). He looks not at what we are, but at what we can be in Him. These are faith words talking.

6:13 Gideon was honest with God. He told Him just how he felt; "If God is with us, then why are we suffering so much?" A lot of people ask these questions. If God is love, why do good people suffer? If I have been serving God, then why am I going through this tough time now?" He asked God "where are all the miracles that you performed with our forefathers in Egypt?" He felt forsaken by God.

6:18-21 God revealed Himself to Gideon as the covenant making God. He showed Gideon Who He is, and He showed Gideon his real position as a covenant partner with God. So often God answers our questions with a revelation of Who He is!

Gideon brought his best to God. Gideon took up his cross. The price of the goat and home baked bread that Gideon brought was extreme for someone in poverty circumstances. Not only that, Gideon cooked soup!

Gideon saw the Cross of Jesus. It could have just been an expensive meal, but God turned it into a covenant meal. In Leviticus 2:1 the meat or meal offering was to be burnt on the altar by the priest. The fact that the Angel of The Lord burned up Gideon's offering with the tip of His staff was a sign of the covenant. I believe that in Gideon's Hebrew mind, he saw a blood covenant that day between himself and God. He saw God exchange power, name and circumstances with him.

The Blood Covenant changes your family, your name, and your inheritance. Gideon received God's name, God took Gideon's name. Mighty Man of Valor: was the Lord's name, defeated weak one was Gideon's name. They swapped.

6:22 Gideon could hear God speak even better now. This was Gideon's main attribute. He took the time to build a relationship and continued to hear God speak. Notice that the Lord had departed in verse 21 yet in verse 23 the Lord spoke. This represents a progressive relationship between Gideon and the Lord.

6:23-24 He had the peace of God because of the Cross (Jehovah-shalom). You can be in terrible circumstances but if you have the peace of God you can overcome anything! "And let the peace of God rule [as an umpire] in your hearts, to which also you were called in one body; and be thankful" (3:15 – comment from Amp. Bible).

6:25-32 Gideon had to tear down family idols. After experiencing the Cross of Jesus we need to tear down the altars. Idolatry is based upon one simple thing; SELF-LOVE. This is more of taking up our cross. Idols are not as obvious today as they were in Old Testament times. An idol is anything that makes you walk in the flesh and not in the Spirit. The most accurate test is what or who do you worship? The most accurate test for worship is whom you obey: Your reasoning, your flesh, another person, or the Spirit of God and the Word of God? Walking in the flesh is obeying your flesh (natural desire) and walking in the Spirit is obeying the Holy Spirit and the Word of God. To pull down idols, one must be in contact with the Word of God and the Holy Spirit so one can cease obeying his/her natural desires.

Like in Romans 12:1 after all of the mercy that God had shown to our lost condition, after the giving of the Cross and all of the grace in Romans chapters 1 through 11, He then says, "In view of all these mercies, offer your own body a living sacrifice." In other words, tear down your idols as Gideon did. Offer all of your faculties to God; give Him your body to be an earthen vessel filled with God as Adam was supposed to be. Be willing to be "different" for God; do not be conformed to this world system.

6:34 After tearing down the idols, Gideon was clothed [possessed] with the Spirit of God. He had the power of God. Gideon had the sense, faith and abandonment to obey God and stop obeying the reasoning and natural circumstances in his life. When we turn from idols we will find the result is always more of the Holy Spirit in our lives. The first thing that happened is that the enemy attacked. When we tear down spiritual idols, we can expect a manifestation of the battle in the natural.

6:36-40 He learned to fellowship with God at a very strong level of trust in spite of circumstances (perhaps even because of them).

Gideon bore fruit for the Kingdom of God. He became one of history's greatest deliverers of God's people. Read Judges 7 through 8:21 for the battle. God turned a defeated man with hopeless circumstances into a great historic victory because of two things: 1) The Cross, and 2) Gideon's appreciation of the Cross to the extent that he would go all out for God and make Him the focus of all of his life, not just first or second place, and Gideon's cooperation to tear down idols and strongholds.

In spite of the fact that Gideon had been subject to family sins, curses and the worshipping of idols, the Angel of the Lord brought the Cross on

55

the scene with the sacrifice, and was saying, "There is no way out for you sonny boy, except that I take on the curse and sin that you have coming to you. By virtue of this covenant, I am taking your sin, your family curses, your generational sins passed down and results of idol worship both by you and your ancestors. I will take your name (your identity) which is 'cursed by God' and you will be called by My Name, O' Mighty Man of Valor." Actually Gideon means "cutter down, hewer."

God met Gideon where he was. God did not require him to be someone he was not. But God had faith in him. Gideon learned that you make it not in your own strength but by

He learned about fruit. He learned that he was a Prisoner in the Promise Land. He learned how to be intimate with God, The Flowing River, and he learned Who God is. He learned to Sit, Walk and Stand. The end result was fruit for the Kingdom of God.

Be desperate to hear God's voice.

Do whatever is necessary to arrange you life to hear God speak. Take time, more and more time, in the Word. Listen to tapes, read good authors, speak the Word, soak in the Word. Take time to be quite with God. Listen more and talk less. Study the Flowing River as a way to hear God's voice more and more. Change your surroundings from time to time, escape from the familiar.

Allow God to speak to your heart!

Chapter 4
Who God is

You can know God.

He wants fellowship with you. God wants you to depend upon being in touch with Him and not depend upon religious acts and duties. To know someone we need to know what his or her character is like. The first thing we need to know about God is that He is the Creator!

Not only is He the Creator, but also by Him, all things still exist and are held together.

Colossians 1:16-17 says, "For all things were created by Him, the things in the heavens, and the things on the earth, the visible and the invisible, whether thrones or dominions or principalities or powers, all things were created through Him and for Him. And He is before all things, and by Him all things consist."

Hebrews 11:3 says, "Through faith we understand that the worlds were framed by the word of God, so that things which are seen were not made of things which do appear."

Hebrews 1:2 (Amplified Bible) says, "But in these last days he has spoken to us in the person of a Son, Whom He appointed Heir and lawful Owner of all things, also by and through Whom He created the worlds and the reaches of space and the ages of time, that is, He made, produced, built, operated and arranged them in order. (verse 3b) .... upholding and maintaining and guiding and propelling the universe by His mighty word of power."

We cannot possibly describe God because He created us.

But here are some other facts about God that we may learn from Scripture:

1. He is uncreated and eternal. (John 1:1-3 and Genesis 21:33).

2. He is all powerful. (Luke 1:37).

3. He is all knowing. (Ps. 147:5).

4. He is ever present. (Jer. 23:23-24).

5. He is a spiritual being. (John 4:24).

6. He is triune, three persons in one. God the Father, the Son, the Holy Spirit. (Matthew 3:16-17, John 1:1-14, 14:9-20).

7. He is infinite. (Isaiah 40:12-13).

8. His nature is love. (Ephesians 2:1-7, 1 John 3:1, 1 John 4:9-10).

God does not HAVE love, He IS love. God loves us with an unconditional love. His love does not depend upon how good or bad we are. While we were dead in sins, He loved us. A dead man cannot do anything but receive life! Humans love with conditions. "If you are good enough, or do what I tell you, then I will love you." Not God! He loves just because He IS love. That is called AGAPE, unconditional love.

9. His character is the fruit of the Sprit described in Galatians 5:22-23.

10. He never changes. His emotions do not run hot and cold like humans. (Hebrews 13:8)

James 1:17 Describes a sun dial shadow that turns as the sun moves during the day. But James says with Jesus, there is NO shadow of turning. In other words, He is always shining like high noon! You can depend upon Him.

11. Jesus is the Word. Jesus is God (John 1:1-2&14).

12. Jesus was born of a virgin. (Luke 1:26-38). Romans 1:3-4 states that: "regarding his Son, who as to his human nature was a descendant of David, and who through the Spirit of holiness was declared with power to be the Son of God, by his resurrection from the dead: Jesus Christ our Lord." Can you imagine asking the teenager Jesus, who are your parents? Jesus might say "Well you see on my mamma's side, I am from the family of David, but on my Dad's side, well, I AM."

13. The Holy Spirit is God. (John 14:16-23, John 16:7-15).

14. Best of all, God is love! He cares about you more than you care about yourself, more than your parents and family cares about you.

The Word of God expresses God's love and concern for you and me in the parables in Luke chapter 15.

No shepherd in his right mind would leave 99 sheep to go after a stray sheep, but God pursues us in our lost state.

The woman in the next parable had lost her hope. The dowry she needed to be married was 10 coins, and she lost one of them. If she did not find it, she would be in poverty or would have to sell her body. God pursues us to make us whole and to fulfill our hopes and dreams.

The Father in the next parable waited on his front porch for his lost son to return. When he saw him a long way off, he did the undignified thing, he ran as fast as he could and covered his dirt so the other servants would not see him; he did not want his son to be embarrassed.

Some common questions about God.

You need to "stop the clock" to understand this.

Does God predestine our lives? Who is in control, God or me, or the world around me? Does God only have certain people who are going to get saved and go to Heaven, and the others have no chance?

Two things to keep in mind:

1. God created man with a free will and He will never violate it.

2. God does not live in time, He lives in eternity. That is not a long time, but it is no time. God knows the beginning from the end and the end from the beginning.

It says in Exodus and Romans 9 that He hardened Pharaoh's heart. Was that fair to Pharaoh? God knew in advance that Pharaoh would not come to Him, therefore, God could justly make him stubborn. Actually, God does not DECIDE to make man stubborn, but there is something inside of man's makeup that makes him stubborn towards God when he rejects God. When we say no to God, something inside of us gets hard, little by little. Finally, we can no longer choose.

God knew this in advance. Did God cause it? NO! Pharaoh's own free choice caused it.

God says in Ephesians 2:10 that our life is predestined for us. Yes, there is a plan for each of our lives, but it is up to us to choose to walk on that path.

God is sovereign, He rules, yet He does it in such a way that does not overwhelm the free will of man, even evil men that plot against God's people and purposes.

Even the people and demons who are God's enemies are working His plan for Him.

Psalm 33:10 says, "The LORD brings the counsel of the nations to nothing; He breaks the plots of the people. The counsel of the LORD stands forever, the thoughts of His heart to all generations."

Psalm 2:1-4 says, "Why do the nations rage, and the peoples meditate on a vain thing? The kings of the earth set themselves, and the rulers plot together, against the LORD and against His anointed, saying, 'Let us break their bands in two and cast away their cords from us.' He who sits in the heavens shall laugh; the LORD shall mock at them."

If you are still having a hard time with this idea, just remember, God lives in Eternity, not time. He looks into our future, our past and our present all at the same time and attempts to bless us with this knowledge. But He will NEVER violate our free will.

God is the Word, and we can trust it (Him).

If there is one thing The Word of God dares to do that no other book in the world does, it is to accurately predict the future.

This proves beyond argument that only God could have authored the Bible.

There are 8,352 verses directly or indirectly concerned with prophecy in Scripture. About one verse in six tells of future events. God's challenge to the world is that we might prove Him. "I am the LORD: I will speak, and the word that I shall speak shall come to pass" (Ezekiel 12:25).

Buddhists, Confucianists and the followers of Mohammed have their sacred writings, but in them the element of prophecy is conspicuous by its absence. The destruction of Tyre, the invasion of Jerusalem, the fall of Babylon and Rome; each was accurately predicted and fulfilled to the smallest of details. The entry of Jesus into Jerusalem was foretold hundreds of years earlier by the prophet Daniel - TO THE VERY DAY! The forming of Israel as a new state in 1948 was foretold to the day and month in the Old Testament.

There are over 300 prophecies that Jesus fulfilled in His birth, life, death, and resurrection. Consider only 17 of the most prominent ones.

The combined probability against these 17 predictions occurring is equal to:

1 chance in 480,000,000,000,000,000,000,000,000,000,000
or 480 Billion X 1 Billion X 1 Trillion.

Concerning the over 300 fulfilled prophecies about Jesus, it is ridiculous to imagine that these prophecies would all be fulfilled by accident by one person. Only one chance in a number followed by 181 zeros! To give you some idea of the size of this immense figure, think of a ball that is packed solidly with electrons (two and a half million billion makes a line about one inch long). Now in your mind imagine this ball expanded to the size of the universe, some four billion light-years in diameter (a light-year being the distance that light travels in a year at the speed of over 186,000 miles per second). Multiply this by 500 quadrillion. Out of this vast container of electrons, remove just **one** electron, and "color" it red and return it to the container. Stir it with the other electrons for a hundred years. Then blindfold a man and send him in to pick it out the first time. Impossible? With the same chance, Jesus the Christ lived, died, was resurrected and is now alive according to the Scriptures by "accident!"

There are many other Old Testament prophecies too numerous to list. There are 1,817 individual prophecies concerning 737 separate subjects found in 8,352 verses. These comprise 27% of the whole of Scriptures.

Isaiah 42:9 says, "Behold, the former things have come to pass, and new things I declare; before they happen, I cause you to hear."

Who is Jesus Now?
In the Gospels, we see who Jesus was when He walked on earth. He showed us the personality of God, His Father. Jesus showed us He was the Lamb of God who took your sin and mine, and Who humbled Himself to suffer the criminal's death on the cross you and I deserved.

The Apostle Paul had a revelation of what Jesus did for us, even though Paul never met Jesus in the flesh. We see those revelations in Paul's epistles.

However, Jesus chose to reveal Himself in a very special way to John.

Notice Revelation 1 verse 1. It says, "The Revelation of Jesus Christ." I believe that God gave us this view of Jesus because we cannot see Him as He really is in any other way. Many walked with Him, many saw Him die, some saw Him resurrected, but no one has really seen Him as He is right now. He is a Warrior, a Judge, the Lamb, Almighty God, He is on the Throne, no being can stand up to Him, He is the Victor, a "terrifying sight" to His enemies, and He is active on your behalf. John needed to know all this.

I believe Jesus showed this vision to John to comfort him by bringing him faith and hope, to make sense of his crazy circumstances, to do the same for the churches to which he wrote this letter almost 2,000 years ago and to do the same for you and me in our lives today when we see all the crazy things going on around us. It is a handbook for obtaining victory in our lives.

John's condition was similar to ours. The world, for John, was going crazy. For some of us, the world is going crazy. Just imagine, he had been living with Jesus for at least 3 years, he saw Him perform mighty miracles, he saw Him crucified, he saw Him resurrected. Certainly, after the resurrection he thought "now there was victory." He saw the Holy Spirit fall on mankind and the start of the church. He established churches and he saw people getting saved. All of the sudden, all of the original disciples were gone and some were crucified; Peter upside down, some were beheaded, others done away with by other means. He saw the world going into a wild spin.

John himself was almost killed by being boiled in oil, but they could not kill him. Now at this time he was taken prisoner and banished forever to the Isle of Patmos (definition = my killing- a rugged and bare island in the Aegean Sea). His daily chore included working a rock quarry and hauling rock up and down hills on his back. He must have thought, "Has the world gone crazy? Did I really know Jesus? Was He really God in the flesh like I wrote about in my Gospel book? Is the church doomed? Is my life wasted?" Then all of the sudden, BAM! Something appeared to him that he had never seen before.

"I came to be in *the* Spirit in the Lord's day and heard behind me a great voice, as of a trumpet, saying, I am the Alpha and Omega, the First and the Last. Also, What you see, write in a book and send *it* to the seven churches which are in Asia: to Ephesus, and to Smyrna, and to Pergamos, and to Thyatira, and to Sardis, and to Philadelphia, and to Laodicea. And I turned to see the voice that spoke with me. And having turned, I saw seven golden lampstands. And in the midst of the seven lampstands I saw *One* like *the* Son of man, clothed with a garment down to *the* feet, and tied around the breast with a golden band. His head and hair *were* white like wool, as white as snow. And His eyes *were* like a flame of fire. And His feet were like burnished brass having been fired in a furnace. And His voice was like the sound of many waters. And He had seven stars in His right hand, and out of His mouth went a sharp two-edged sword. And His face *was* like the sun shining in its strength. And when I saw Him, I fell at His feet as dead. And He laid His right hand upon me, saying to me, 'Do not fear, I am the First and the Last, and the Living One, and I became dead, and behold, I am alive for ever and ever, Amen. And I have the keys of hell and of death'" (Revelation 1:10-18).

Christ Revealed

In Revelation chapter 1 John sees Who Jesus is now! He is different from the last time he saw Him. He is the ascended Christ revealed! He is revealed as the faithful, trustworthy witness, the firstborn of the dead, the Prince of the Kings of the Earth, the soon coming One, and the Alpha and Omega, the first and last, the Almighty Omnipotent One!

He is revealed as the one who is coming to judge His church with fire in His eyes, a golden girdle, and feet that shined as burnished brass. This judgment is not to condemn the church, but to protect it from the coming wrath. Holiness is what will protect the church!

In Revelation chapters 2-3 Jesus is speaking to the church, both then and now, as if a general was speaking to his troops getting them ready for battle. Because a major conflict was soon to occur, and the seven churches would be destroyed if not prepared, Jesus addressed each church according to its own shortcoming. He encouraged them to get in right standing with God. Holiness is what will protect the church!

In Revelation 4, Jesus invites John, and you and me, to come up into the heavenlies to see the events from His vantage point. We need to see events in life from God's perspective. We can get so earthly minded, and our sight can be so horizontal in looking at our circumstances that we miss seeing things from God's point of view. We are sitting in the heavenlies with Christ, therefore, the Holy Spirit can give us that view. When we see our circumstances from God's vantage point, they do not seem as bad.

In Revelation 5, God is the one who originates the battles. Satan does not originate battles in our lives. Notice, no one was worthy to unroll the scroll and take off the seals except for Jesus, as the Lion of the Tribe of Judah and at the same time the Lamb of God. Jesus is the Lion or the victor and most powerful force. Jesus is the Lamb, the one who takes what we have coming. We could not stand in the difficult circumstances of life except that Jesus, as the Lamb, takes what we have coming!

Jesus is the one who originates battles. We need to keep this in mind when trouble comes. It may be an evil attack, but it is Jesus who has put a hook in the nose of our enemies to come at us so that we may destroy them in His name! Blessed be the Name of the Lord forever!!! Hallelujah!

In Revelation 5-16, there is great war, conflict, judgment and persecution as the scroll is unfurled. Things are going crazy, and events go from bad to worse to almost intolerable. But in this, God is looking for those who will overcome and stand.

Revelation 7:3 shows that those believers who are faithful in this overcoming process are stamped by God for safe keeping. Things are going to get worse!

A parenthetical statement is made in Revelation 11 showing the victory of the Cross and showing that the dominion of the world's system has been given to the Kingdom of God and the Lord Jesus Christ.

Revelation 12:11 shows us that if we stand during this time of great trouble that we will overcome the enemy by the blood of the Lamb and by the Word of God being testified by our mouths, provided that we do not love our own lives more than we love God and His purposes.

Revelation 17 is the revelation of the "world" system and its corruption. It shows the cooperation between the spiritual and the political.

Revelation 18 is another warning to God's people to come out of the "world" system because it is about to be destroyed and it is unreliable. The destruction of this system is demonstrated.

In Revelation 19 there is victory, and the Lord returns on His white horse to fulfill His promise and to bring His rewards. "And I saw Heaven opened. And behold, a white horse! And He sitting on him *was* called Faithful and True. And in righteousness He judges and makes war. And His eyes *were* like a flame of fire, and on His head many crowns. And He had a name written, one that no one knew except Himself. And He had been clothed *in* a garment dipped in blood, and His name is called The Word of God. And the armies in Heaven followed Him on white horses, clothed in fine linen, white and clean. And out of His mouth goes a sharp sword, so that with it He should strike the nations. And He will shepherd them with a rod of iron. And He treads the winepress of the wine of the anger and of the wrath of Almighty God. And He has on *His* garment, and on His thigh a name written, *KING OF KINGS AND LORD OF LORDS*" (Revelation 19:11-16).

In Revelation 20, Satan is bound; judgment takes place.

Revelation 21 shows the Kingdom of God becoming more real, the New Jerusalem. It shows a deeper intimacy with Jesus as a result of all we have been through.

Revelation 22 shows ministry for those people who have stood and overcome to the end. Here is a picture of the Flowing River, mentioned in Ezekiel 47, with fruit on both sides for the healing of the nations, meaning the gentiles, or the people who do not know God. In my experience, real ministry comes after much tribulation and overcoming. We take dominion over demons through the battles.

Revelation 22 is also a word of encouragement. "I am coming quickly, hang on and you will be blessed. Hang on and you will turn all this tribulation and trouble in your life into a blessing."

This revelation or glorification of Jesus Christ most likely is similar to what Jesus spoke to the two on the Road to Emmaus, and later to the 11 disciples, from Moses, the Psalms and the Prophets in Luke 24. Most likely, however, this was a more complete revelation. When we see Jesus glorified in this way, we are candidates for the filling of the Holy Spirit (John 7:39).

I do not pretend to understand all of the Book of Revelation, nor do I claim to do a complete teaching on it here. Neither am I saying that it does not apply to future world prophecy and events. All I am saying is that it is

MORE than that. It is an important application for our lives today. We need to know who Jesus is NOW! I also know that on August 26, 1979, while reading the Book of Revelation, Jesus miraculously saved me and filled me with the Holy Spirit. He revealed Himself to me and I have never been the same!

John then understood. There is more to life than just making it to Heaven and living a good life here. We are called to be in a war, and Jesus is alive and powerful to make sure we get the victory! This is a picture for us to understand when things are not going well. We need to place ourselves somewhere in this process and know that it is God ordained. Then we can stand!

Here you have the first picture of God. He is uncreated. He always existed, He never did not exist. He will never cease to exist. He is all powerful, He knows all because He lives outside of time in eternity. He knows the future because to Him it has already happened. He is all knowing. He can read your mind, He knows what you are going to think before you think it. He is present everywhere through the Holy Spirit.

He is God the Father, Jesus the Son who is also called the Word of God, and God the Holy Spirit .

He is ruler over all. He is the victor over all enemies. All things are in His hands!

You can trust Him and His Word no matter what! God is awesome! We cannot begin to understand how great He is! He loves us beyond what we can imagine!

Chapter 5
Sit

 Sitting has to do with our self-image and who we are in Christ. The Devil can kill, steal and destroy us if our conduct and lifestyle is not pleasing to the Lord. However, what we think of ourselves, or our self- image determines our conduct. We may try hard to change our conduct, but it is really determined by our self-image. What we think of ourselves (our self-image) is the only thing we can change. In order to have an accurate image of ourselves (accurate in God's eyes), we must renew our minds by the Word of God. "And do not be conformed to this world, but be transformed by the renewing of your mind, in order to prove by you what is that good and pleasing and perfect will of God" (Romans 12:2).

If you want to have a fruit bearing abundant life, you will need to know how these three issues SIT, WALK and STAND, work together.

We need to STAND against the Devil - (warfare - John 10:10). Satan is determined to steal your seed as described in Mark chapter 4.

But we cannot STAND until we learn how to WALK - (our conduct or lifestyle - Ephesians 4:27). Satan will attempt to cause you to walk out your life in an ungodly manner so that you will be unable to STAND against him with the power of Jesus, who is holy.

However, we cannot WALK until we learn to SIT - (our self-image - Luke 6:45). Many Christians attempt to walk out a holy life by self-determination, which eventually becomes legalism and rules. This style of life will cut you off from real time relationship with the Lord Jesus.

We are living in a spiritual war and we need to STAND against the enemy, but we cannot stand unless we are living the right life and we cannot live the right life if we have the wrong self-image.

We need to know who we are (SIT) before we can live as we should (WALK), and before we can (STAND) against the Devil in our lives. This is based upon three verses in Ephesians:

SIT - Ephesians 2:5-6 says, "(even when we were dead in sins) has made us alive together with Christ (by grace you are saved), and has raised us up together and made us *sit* together in the heavenlies in Christ Jesus."

According to this verse, are we are SITTING with Christ in the heavenlies; or are we going to after we die and go to Heaven?

WALK - Ephesians 4:1 says, "I therefore, the prisoner in the Lord, beseech you that you *walk* worthy of the calling with which you are called."

STAND - Ephesians 6:11 says, "Put on the whole armor of God so that you may be able to *stand* against the wiles of the devil."

Let us learn to sit.

We are going to behave exactly like what our heart tells us we are. "The good man brings good things out of the good stored up in his heart, and the evil man brings evil things out of the evil stored up in his heart. For out of the overflow of his heart his mouth speaks" (Luke 6:45).

To SIT with Christ in Heavenly Places depends upon His Cross.

Look again at Ephesians 2:5. It says that we were dead in our sins. Can a dead man do anything? No way. A dead man does not need to learn to walk or stand, or to throw away bad habits, a dead man needs LIFE ! A dead man cannot give himself life, he cannot even try. It took God through Christ to give us life.

First, let's define sit in terms of the spiritual world.

Our legs are holding us when we stand, but when we sit we are resting our weight on the chair. It is a matter of effort or rest. We either become weary or rested. We rest our entire weight on Jesus, our very selves, and our very future.

In creation, God did everything before He created us. Adam began his life with the Sabbath. What did man have to do with the creation in the first 6 days? How much help did God receive from Adam in creating the heavens and the earth? What was Adam's first day like? It was a day of rest. Read Genesis 1. God created everything in 5 days, then He created man on the 6th day. Man did not help God. The first day that man awakened to was the 7th day, which was the day of rest. Only after Adam was totally provided for did he go to work.

God worked, then rested. Man rests, then works.

This is the Gospel! God completed the work of redemption. He purchased us from bondage to sin and Satan and gave us a new nature, a new birth that implanted the very life and character of God inside of us. We could do nothing to earn this. All we can do is enter in by faith when we hear about the offer.

You may or may not feel different, but your feelings are not reliable. You need to become accustomed to believing God's Word and put your emotions and feelings aside. Some wonderful and beautiful events have taken place in the life of a Christian. The enemy, Satan, will use your old sense ruled mind to hide those facts from you. They are facts, they can be relied on. When we begin to take the Word of God as final authority, we will begin to see the truth. Final authority is not circumstances, it is not your emotions, it is God's Word. Take a journey into the Word of God to see who you are!

There is a legal side and an experiential side to who you are. When you submitted to Jesus as Lord, and when God planted the Word of God in your heart, you entered into the death and resurrection of Jesus. You experienced the new birth. 1 Peter 1:23 says, "having been born again, not of corruptible seed, but of incorruptible, through the living word of God, and abiding forever."

Legally, we have been crucified with Christ according to Galatians 2:20 and Romans 6:6. Galatians 2:20 says, "I have been crucified with Christ, and I live; yet no longer I, but Christ lives in me. And that life I now live in the flesh, I live by faith toward the Son of God, who loved me and gave Himself on my behalf."

However, we may not be experiencing that reality as yet. This is where so many new believers get on the wrong track. Just because they are not experiencing the truth in the Word, or worse, they may be experiencing the opposite of what the Word says, they become discouraged and quit believing. In the world, seeing is believing, but with God, you must believe before you will ever see.

We need to know that we are not two people, we do not have dual personalities! Some Christians promote this idea due to their experience of not having victory over sin. Some say that Paul's dialog in Romans 7 indicates that we have two natures living in us. Romans 7 does not say that. It says that the "sin principle" is working in us. If we have been crucified with Christ and born again, then the old nature, the old man has died, and a new man has been born in us.

We need to renew our minds. When we are born again, our spirits are regenerated, when we go to Heaven our bodies we will renewed, but our minds are renewed daily as we live out the Word of God. The answer to the struggle is as our Pastor put it into perspective during a service. He said that we are not freaks, two people, but rather our "flesh" is really the old thinking in our brain and mind. Our minds have old "tapes" that cause us to act according to the old nature. It is kind of like a tree that has been chopped down but all the leaves have not died as yet. The Scripture that supports this is Romans 12:1-2 which says, "Therefore, I urge you, brothers, in view of God's mercy, to offer your bodies as living sacrifices, holy and pleasing to God--this is your spiritual act of worship. Do not conform any longer to the pattern of this world, but be transformed by the renewing of your mind. Then you will be able to test and approve what God's will is--his good, pleasing and perfect will."

Jesus became your sin and you became His righteousness.

II Corinthians 5:21 says, "For he hath made him to be sin for us, who knew no sin; that we might be made the righteousness of God in him."

How did this happen? A blood covenant has been applied to your life. A great exchange has taken place between you and Jesus Christ. On the cross, He took every bad and negative thing in your life. At the resurrection He gave you every positive thing in the nature of God Almighty! He begot you as sons and daughters and seated you with Him in a realm FAR above all your enemies. Satan, your enemy, will do all in his power to steal this from you with lies. However, if you know the truth, and stand on the truth, you will be a winner! You went through the crucifixion with Him, the death with Him and have already been resurrected with Him.

We must look at how Jesus came to this place of sitting. He was crucified, dead, buried and resurrected. At His resurrection He became the first born of a new creation. After His disciples and about 500 others saw him for many days, He went back to the right hand of the Father, and was seated as King and ruler of the universe.

Now, if we are sitting with Him in the heavenlies, then it stands to reason that we went through the entire process with Him, death, burial, and resurrection to a new creation and ascension. It is like putting a marker in a book, and then moving the book around. The marker goes with it. You may ask, "how can I have experienced this process with Christ, I was not even alive then?"

The answer to that lies in the fact that God lives in eternity, which really is the absence of time. So when we experience the new birth, we pick up the entire history of Jesus, no matter what the time difference may be. Some Scriptures for this are:

"how much more shall the blood of Christ (who through the eternal Spirit offered Himself unblemished spot to God) purge your conscience from dead works to serve the living God?" (Hebrews 9:14).

"(this) grace which was given us in Christ Jesus before the eternal times" (2 Timothy 1:9b).

Following are some facts in the Word that you should meditate on. These facts are good seed, which will bear good fruit in your life. The Holy Spirit through the Word can make who you are in Christ a reality. You need to take the Word at face value and believe it as a legal document.

You were hopelessly lost. That means that someone else had to search for you. Ephesians 2:12 (a & b) says, "that at that time you were without Christ, ...having no hope and without God in the world."

You were dead in your sins. There is no way out for a dead man, except to receive life. Ephesians 2:1 says, "And you He made alive, who were dead in trespasses and sins."

The blood Jesus shed on the Cross removed your sins. He took your place. Colossians 1:14 says, "in whom we have redemption through His blood, the remission of sins." Ephesians 1:7 says, "In Him we have redemption through His blood, the forgiveness of sins, according to the riches of His grace." The word, "forgiveness," actually means to separate or cut away. Our sins have been taken away from us and put on to Jesus, our sacrificial Lamb.

You were already "In Christ" when the following events took place.

You were crucified with Christ. "I have been crucified with Christ; it is no longer I who live, but Christ lives in me; and the life which I now live in the flesh I live by faith in the Son of God, who loved me and gave Himself for me" (Galatians 2:20).

You died with Christ. "For if we have been joined together in the likeness of His death, we shall also be in the likeness of His resurrection" (Romans 6:5).

You were buried with Christ. "We were buried therefore with Him through Baptism into death" (Romans 6:4). "Having been buried with him in baptism" (Colossians 2:12).

You were made alive with Christ. "And you being dead through your trespasses and the uncircumcision of your flesh, you did He make alive together with Him" (Colossians 2:13). "Even when we were dead through our trespasses [God] made us alive together with Christ" (Ephesians 2:5).

You were raised with Christ. You are seated with Christ. "[He God] made us alive with Christ even when we were dead in transgressions-- it is by grace you have been saved. And God raised us up with Christ and seated us with him in the heavenly realms in Christ Jesus" (Ephesians 2:5,6).

That is our legal standing with God today and the foundation of our legal rights. As far as the spiritual world is concerned, your position is with Christ in the heavenlies. You are in a seat of authority. Satan and your mind will tell you that you are not seated with Christ in the heavenlies, but that is a lie! You need to know that God seated you with Him while you were yet a sinner!

You are a new creation. "Therefore, if anyone is in Christ, he is a new creation; old things have passed away; behold, all things have become new"(2 Corinthians 5:17).

You might ask, how can this be? Good question. God put us in Christ. "But of Him you are in Christ Jesus, who became for us wisdom from God--and righteousness and sanctification and redemption" (1 Corinthians 1:30). Being in Christ is like you were in your father and mother as a sperm and an egg. You inherited their history in your genealogy. Just imagine that you are a marker inside of a book. When the book is moved, the marker goes with it. When the book is put on the shelf, the marker goes on the shelf. If the book is burned, the marker is burned. If by some miracle the book is restored and put back on the shelf, so is the marker.

Your history, and who you are in Christ is the result of the Blood Covenant with God through Jesus' death on the Cross and His resurrection.

You are righteous. Righteous means to have a right standing with God. A son (or daughter) is righteous with his father by birth. He is in the family and he has a right standing that the neighbor does not have. We are righteous by our new birth, not by anything we have done. "God made him who had no sin to be sin for us, so that in him we might become the righteousness of God" (2 Corinthians 5:21). We are righteous because God put His life in us, not because of the way we act or live.

Satan's dominion over you is broken. Satan had dominion of your old nature, but your new nature is Christ's own Spirit that has already defeated Satan. Romans 6:8-10 says, "But if we died with Christ, we believe that we shall also live with Him, knowing that when Christ was raised from the dead, He dies no more; *death no longer has dominion* over Him. For in that He died, He died to sin once; but in that He lives, He lives to God." If the spirit world has had you living in fear, God will set you free right now!

We need a renewing of the mind.

"Therefore, I urge you, brothers, in view of God's mercy, to offer your bodies as living sacrifices, holy and pleasing to God--this is your spiritual act of worship. Do not conform any longer to the pattern of this world, but be transformed by the renewing of your mind. Then you will be able to test and approve what God's will is--his good, pleasing and perfect will" (Romans 12:1-2).

Here is God's promise to you. Hebrews 8:10 says, "For this *is* the covenant that I will make with the house of Israel after those days, saith the Lord; I will put my laws into their mind, and write them in their hearts: and I will be to them a God, and they shall be to me a people."

Read 1 Peter 1:6-7. What does it say about testing and trials?

The proof of whether or not you believe is NOT how you feel. The proof is what will come out of your mouth from the abundance of your heart. Luke 6:45 says, "A good man out of the good treasure of his heart brings forth the good. And an evil man out of the evil treasure of his heart brings forth the evil. For out of the abundance of the heart his mouth speaks."

The only way to overcome and be healed from things like sin, fear, guilt, addictions, feeling unworthy, feeling like a failure, etc. is to accept these facts. When we know for sure that God loves us, that we belong to Him, that He has made us a new creation and old things have passed away and we know that our new identity is in Christ, that we have been purchased from slavery and been given the choice to accept the absolute Lordship, authority and care of God, that is when we begin the process of overcoming all the bad things in our life.

The easiest thing to remember is the Cross. The Cross of Jesus took everything that is bad in our life and that comes into our life, and transforms it into a blessing.

All this fantastic and good news of who we are should not give us a proud, puffed up attitude. "I am the vine, ye are the branches"(John 15:5). Without absolute dependence upon the life of God living in us, we are nothing. We are not called upon to be independent power people. We are called upon to be totally dependent upon the life that was inserted into us. A branch cannot do anything, it will die, if it does not stay united with the vine. We need to take on the cloak of humility and know that without Him we are nothing! If you examine John 15, staying dependent is always related to the Word of God.

70

Don't be a chicken, you are an eagle!
One day, an eagle's egg fell from its nest and rolled into a chicken pen. The eagle was born with the chickens and acted like a chicken, but it kept seeing a difference as it grew. No one was there to tell it that it was not a chicken, but an eagle.

When storms came, the eagle would rush off to the chicken house with the rest of the chickens, running for cover, but the eagle always looked over his shoulder and up, and he saw these other strange birds on the cliff. They were not afraid, they were not running. They were standing with their wings locked into special sockets (that make them like a wing welded to the fuselage of an airplane), they gazed right into the storm even though it was still miles away. They waited and waited and then, bang! The storm hit them but instead of hurting them all it did was make them soar. They went straight up into the air, up to 30,000 feet above the storm into clear air. The eagle would say to himself, "oh man look at those guys, I wish I were like them."

One day he looked UP, and saw an eagle flying and soaring high with a storm. All of the sudden he knew, "I am not a chicken, I am an eagle. Why should I run?" He climbed the hill, locked his wings, then he took off and soared!

My friend, you are not a mere human, you are not a chicken. You are made to soar in the heavenlies with Christ. Look up!

Now remember the parable of the sower in Mark 4 (read it). Satan comes to steal the seed of the Word of God sown in your heart. Today a seed of who you are was sown. Tomorrow, stand fast if discouragement comes through some circumstance. The Word is true! Circumstances come and go.

Quote From Richard Wurmbrand's devotional, <u>Reaching Towards the Heights</u> - May 15th. (5)
"We become holy by feeding upon the right spiritual food.
In an experiment it was found that worms that usually live in the darkness can be conditioned to leave this habitat and to prefer the light. As often as they would withdraw into darkness, they would get electric shocks, whereas if they came out in the light, they found abundant food. With time, these beings 'put on a new worm,' to use the biblical expression. Contrary to the habits of their species, from that time on they preferred the light to darkness. Then these worms were cut into small pieces and added in the food given to other worms: and, lo, these worms also changed their habits. They had increased, with the addition of the flesh of the new breed of worms, their Ribonucleic acid (RNA), the depository of memory. They would shun darkness and prefer light just as the beings upon which they had fed. Similar experiments have also been made with other animals.

If you wish to put on the new man, a man of righteousness and holiness, feed upon Christ. He has become flesh in order that He might become your daily food."

On the Cross, Jesus quoted from Psalm 22:6 "I am a worm."

Strong's concordance[2] definition for worm: 08438 elwt towla` {to-law'}.

from 03216; TWOT - 2516b; n mAV - scarlet 34, worm 8, crimson - the female 'coccus ilicis' 1b) scarlet stuff, crimson, scarlet 1b1) the dye made from the dried body of the female of the worm "coccus ilicis"

When the female of the scarlet worm species was ready to give birth to her young, she would attach her body to the trunk of a tree, fixing herself so firmly and permanently that she would never leave again. The eggs deposited beneath her body were thus protected until the larvae were hatched and able to enter their own life cycle. As the mother died, the crimson fluid stained her body and the surrounding wood. From the dead bodies of such female scarlet worms, the commercial scarlet dyes of antiquity were extracted.

What a picture this gives of Christ, dying on the tree, shedding his precious blood that he might "bring many sons unto glory" (Heb 2:10)! He died for us, that we might live through him!

Chapter 6
Walk

 We cannot Stand unless we Walk.
Our enemy will "eat us for lunch." Here are some Scriptures that back this up.

"Put on the whole armor of God, that you may be able to stand against the wiles of the devil. For we do not wrestle against flesh and blood, but against principalities, against powers, against the rulers of the darkness of this age, against spiritual hosts of wickedness in the heavenly places" (Ephesians 6:11,12).

"Lest Satan should get an advantage of us: for we are not ignorant of his devices" (2 Corinthians 2:11).

"Neither give place to the devil"(Ephesians 4:27).

"He must also have a good reputation with outsiders, so that he will not fall into disgrace and into the devil's trap" (1 Timothy 3:7).

"and that they will come to their senses and escape from the trap of the devil, who has taken them captive to do his will" (2 Timothy 2:26).

"Be self-controlled and alert. Your enemy the devil prowls around like a roaring lion looking for someone to devour" (1 Peter 5:8).

It is clear from these Scriptures and many others, that even as believers we can become the victim of Satan and his assistants in many different ways. These Scriptures also show that our conduct and lifestyle have something to do with giving Satan the right to hurt us.

Our victory over Satan and circumstances can only be successful as a result of our *walk*. We need the character of Jesus in our lives to be safe. If we attempt to make it in life with our old character, we have already lost the spiritual war. However, if we are walking in God's character, then the enemy only sees Jesus and not us. Remember, the enemy has no place in Jesus. Jesus already defeated Satan.

Ephesians 4:1 says, "I therefore, the prisoner in the Lord, beseech you that you walk worthy of the calling with which you are called."

We sought to make it clear in the "Sit" lesson that our self-image determines our conduct, and that the Christian life does not begin with "walking." In other words our performance, or anything that we can do or accomplish. Grace is what got us in, and grace is what will carry us through!

Everything is based upon the finished work of Jesus at the Cross of Calvary and what He accomplished there and who we became as a result of His cross.

The Lord has done everything for us. He is seated at the throne and we are seated with Him. We have been crucified, we died, were buried, were raised and resurrected with Him and we have been seated with Him in the heavenlies. Ephesians 2:6 says, "and has raised us up together and made us sit together in the heavenlies in Christ Jesus."

However, the Christian life does not end there. Our Christian walk is a relationship between two persons, God and us. A relationship does not come instantly, it requires much time. Therein lies the problem with most Christians. They do not wish to take time, to give their priority to keeping their relationship living and vital with God. Romans 12:1-2 makes it clear that in view of the wonderful mercies of God that we need now to respond by offering ourselves a living sacrifice, which is our reasonable service. In thus doing we constantly renew our minds from the old way of living and the result and promise is that we will prove, or walk out, the will of God for our lives.

To walk worthy of the Lord depends upon our cross. Luke 9:23 says, "And He said to all, If anyone desires to come after Me, let him deny himself and take up his cross daily and follow Me."

Remember, our relationship with God is a blood covenant. It takes two parties and two deaths to make it valid.

There are several types of choices we have daily. Depending upon our choice, we either get closer or further from God.

a. Moral choices. Do we say yes or no to stealing, lying, cheating, illicit sex, gossip and the list goes on? Are we obeying the Word, or our flesh?

b. Trials and suffering. Do we say yes or no to trusting in God's Word more than our circumstances? Are we trusting the Word or our flesh?

c. Authority. Do we say yes or no the Lordship of Jesus and the Holy Spirit? Do we say yes or no to the authorities that God puts over us, like teachers, pastors, police, parents, etc.? If you cannot obey who is over you, then leave. If they are asking you to sin, then do not obey them. God will protect you from even evil authority.

d. The World. Do we say yes or no to the *world*? The *world* is a spiritual kingdom just like the Kingdom of God. 1 John 2:15-16 says the craving for sensual gratification, the greedy longings of the mind and the assurance in one's own resources are attributes of the "world" (Lust of the flesh, lust of the eyes, pride of life). Each time we choose one of these, we move away from God.

We are not perfect, but we can walk and live in repentance. We will fail from time to time, but God gives us a perfect forgiveness, just as we had never sinned. 1 John 1:9 says, "if we confess our sins, He is faithful and just to forgive us our sins, and to cleanse us from all unrighteousness."

God knows that most of us fail not because we want to, but because we are victims of something. His cure is not to slap us around, but to come and let us know who we are in Him, with the hope that will cause us to be drawn to Him even more.

Don't be like Esau. He was Jacob's twin brother. Esau, on the surface did not seem any worse than his twin brother Jacob. Jacob was a deceiver, yet God intervened and supernaturally gave the first born birthright to Jacob, even though Jacob was the last one out of the womb. Esau despised his birthright, thinking that it was not that big of a deal, and sold it to Jacob for a bowl of stew. Yet later in life when he tried to repent, he could not. We have a spiritual birthright when we are born of God, and this is a warning to us not to despise it. We could end up as Esau, who did not make it (Hebrews 12:16).

Walking in the Spirit

Galatians 5:16 says, "I say, then, Walk in the Spirit and you shall not fulfill the lusts of the flesh."

Romans 8:1 says, "There is therefore now no condemnation to those who are in Christ Jesus, who walk not according to the flesh but according to the Spirit."

Walking in the Spirit is a simple, but different way to live and the easiest way I know to be right with God on a daily basis. It is a process that goes like this:

1. You continue to look into the Word of God (mirror) and ask God to show you how to live. Ask Him, and seek out what His standards are for your life. For instance, it says to not lie, to treat your friends with love, to submit to your parents and teachers, to treat your brothers and sisters with kindness, to not get drunk, do not be selfish, don't be angry, always forgive not matter what, etc.

2. You determine to live the way God wants you to, knowing that only God in you can walk a life worthy of the Lord.

3. When you fail, and you will, be totally honest with yourself, God and others around you. Repent (turn) quickly. The promise is that when we repent (turn) that the Kingdom of God is at hand, or within our reach.

4. Confess your sin to God. 1 John 1:9 says, "If we confess our sins, He is faithful and just to forgive us our sins, and to cleanse us from all unrighteousness."

5. Confess what the Word of God says about your situation in a positive way, i.e., Galatians 2:20 that says, "I have been crucified with

Christ, and I live; yet no longer I, but Christ lives in me. And that life I now live in the flesh, I live by faith toward the Son of God, who loved me and gave Himself on my behalf."

6. As you continue to live this way those old habits and old sinful ways begin to disappear. The grace of God takes over and gives you the character of God instead of your old character.

7. Grace kicks in for your sin. You did not get righteous by the things you did, so your righteousness is still there, it just has some dirt on it.

While you walk in the Spirit, God gives you grace for your mistakes, and takes the penalty of the sin that you would normally suffer, and gives you a blessing that you do not deserve.

8. Not only does grace kick in for your sin, not only does God give you a blessing that you did not deserve, but the grace you receive is actually the power that gets rid of the sin (or the problem) you are dealing with in the first place. Look at Zechariah 4:7 which says, "Who *art* thou, O great mountain? before Zerebbabel [a type of Jesus] *thou shalt become* a plain: and he shall bring forth the headstone *thereof with* shoutings, *crying,* Grace, grace unto it." God speaks "grace" to your situation, and the mountain is removed!

David was called a man after God's own heart, even after he sinned tragically with Bathsheba and Uriah. You may find yourself in this place. If you do, you need to recall that David not only confessed his sin to God, but as is stated in his repentance in Psalm 51, he asked God to give him a pure heart and to renew a right spirit within him. God knows if you really want to change like David did.

The Word judges us. You need to look into the mirror.

James 1:23-25 says, "Anyone who listens to the word but does not do what it says is like a man who looks at his face in a mirror and, after looking at himself, goes away and immediately forgets what he looks like. But the man who looks intently into the perfect law that gives freedom, and continues to do this, not forgetting what he has heard, but doing it--he will be blessed in what he does."

The Word of God is our judge just like a mirror is our judge. It looks at us and tells us the truth of what is right and what is wrong. But we can look at a some dirt on our face, see it, and walk away and forget it. James says we can do the same thing when we look at the Word of God. We can see what we are supposed to do, but we can walk away as if we never saw it. If the man who obeys is blessed, then the man who does not obey is cursed!

Obedience to the Word is a powerful thing!

1. It "takes up your cross," it completes the blood covenant and puts you under the care and protection of God.

2. It totally takes Satan off your case. He will still attempt to hurt you, bad things may seem to happen, but they cannot hurt you. Matthew 7:24-27

says, "Therefore everyone who hears these words of mine and puts them into practice is like a wise man who built his house on the rock. The rain came down, the streams rose, and the winds blew and beat against that house; yet it did not fall, because it had its foundation on the rock. But everyone who hears these words of mine and does not put them into practice is like a foolish man who built his house on sand. The rain came down, the streams rose, and the winds blew and beat against that house, and it fell with a great crash."

3. It prepares you for eternity. The more you obey, the more Jesus gives you His Spirit and makes Himself real to you. Also, something happens inside of you over a period of time that separates you from the world and makes you closer to Jesus. When you get to Heaven, you will have a position closer to Him forever!

4. There are always rewards for obedience to His Word. John 14:23 tells us that our reward is His presence. Jesus draws us into His presence and we experience eternity, we are partakers of the Divine Nature!

5. You become a slave to whom you obey. Will it be Jesus or someone else? Romans 6:16 says, "Don't you know that when you offer yourselves to someone to obey him as slaves, you are slaves to the one whom you obey-- whether you are slaves to sin, which leads to death, or to obedience, which leads to righteousness?"

Obedience to God is not based upon the fear that He will hurt you if you disobey; it is based upon the fact that you love Him and want to please Him. John 14:21 says, "Whoever has my commands and obeys them, he is the one who loves me. He who loves me will be loved by my Father, and I too will love him and show myself to him."

If you want to see who loves God, look around and see who is going out of their way to obey Him!

Now let's look at the mirror. (Please refer to A Spiritual Check-up in the Flowing River chapter.

Chapter 7
Stand

I am defeated
when a believer
Stands!

Have you ever purchased something that did not work and then try to take it back to the store? That is what so many Christians do. They hear the Good News and then they don't wait long enough to see it become real in their own life, and they return it as something that does not work!

Sometimes it is difficult to believe the truth we cannot see and feel with our five natural senses. There can be no victory without conflict.

We must recognize that we dwell in an enemy's territory. His aim is to keep lost people lost and going to Hell. His aim for Christians is to get them so interested in the Kingdom of the World and its systems of money, entertainment, power, popularity, etc., so that they are not even aware that they could live by a higher kingdom, the Kingdom of God. Satan does not always use "bad" things to tempt us, sometimes he uses the "good" things of the world to lure us away from God's Kingdom.   Satan uses circumstances and ideas to convince us that we are not SITTING with Christ, that we should not WALK like He walks and that we should give up instead of STANDING on the promises. We are heirs of the Kingdom of God, so why should we live like those people who are not?

Standing against the wiles of the devil.

Ephesians 6:11 says, "Put on the whole armor of God so that you may be able to stand against the wiles of the devil."

Now that we understand Sitting (who we are in Christ), and Walking (living a life worthy of the Lord), we are prepared for spiritual conflict, which is called Standing.

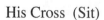

I am
defeated!

His Cross (Sit)　　　　　+　　Your cross (Walk)　　=　　Victory

God's plan to take care of all of your needs is to give you fruit from the seed of the Word. Satan's plan is to block that fruit by stealing the seed and/or making you unfruitful. Standing is the final step in bearing fruit for your life. Standing is only for those who have received SIT and WALK. Standing means to hang on with patience, faithfulness, perseverance, and to speak faith words no matter how bad circumstances look and no matter how bad you feel. It means to practice what you learned in Sitting and Walking every day.

Here is how it works:
Jesus was teaching His disciples in Mark chapter 4. He told them that *the mystery* (not one of the mysteries, but *the mystery*) of the Kingdom of God was contained in this parable. He asked them in verse 13, "And He said to them, 'Do you not know this parable? And how then will you know all parables?'" Jesus used this very visible agricultural example of seed being sown to explain and unveil the mystery of the unseen world. Mark 4:9-11 says, "And He said to them, 'He who has ears to hear, let him hear.' And when He was alone, they who were about Him, with the Twelve, asked Him concerning the parable. And He said to them, 'To you it is given to know the mystery of the kingdom of God. But to those outside, all *these* things are *given* in parables.'"

The entire Kingdom of God works like this parable. God plants the seeds of His Words in our hearts (regardless of the condition of our heart). These seeds represent all of God's purposes for our lives, beginning from being born again, to being filled with the Spirit, to being healed physically and mentally, being provided for, bringing us into our proper relationships in life, and everything else that is God's purposes for us. It all works by the seed of the Word being planted.

Mark 4:14-20 says, "The sower sows the Word. And these are those by the wayside, where the Word is sown. And when they hear, Satan comes immediately and takes away the Word that was sown in their hearts. And these are those likewise being sown on stony places; who, when they hear the Word, immediately receive it with gladness. But they have no root in themselves, but are temporary. Afterward when affliction or persecution arises for the Word's sake, they are immediately offended. And these are those being sown among thorns; such as hear the Word, and the cares of this world, and the deceit of riches, and the lust about other things entering in, choke the Word, and it becomes unfruitful. And these are those sown on good ground, who hear the Word and welcome *it*, and bear fruit, one thirty, one sixty, and one a hundredfold."

Notice that Satan comes to steal the Word. This is really the only weapon that Satan has against mankind; to steal the Word or to blind us from the Word (2 Corinthians 4:4). If any person would receive the Word of God, they would be saved and go to Heaven. If any person would receive and believe the Word of God, they would be made whole, their needs would be provided, and their life would be in order. Satan cannot hurt anyone who believes the Word of God. He can and does tempt them, he can put signs on them that make it look like the Word is not true, but he cannot hurt you if you are totally submitted to the Lordship of the Word, Who is Jesus Himself!

We will always need to overcome difficulties, but we can overcome and win. The way in which we overcome, the results, are God's business. Often things do not work out according to our plans. However, we can trust Him in all things!

If Satan can get you to act according to your old nature (flesh) and the way of the world, he can steal God's promises. Galatians 5:19-21 says, "Now the works of the flesh are clearly revealed, which are: adultery, fornication, uncleanness, lustfulness, idolatry, sorcery, hatreds, fightings, jealousies, angers, rivalries, divisions, heresies, envyings, murders, drunkennesses, revelings, and things like these; of which I tell you before, as I also said before, that they who do such things shall not inherit the kingdom of God." (The seed of the Word bearing fruit in your life.)

So in a very simple, childlike way of looking at spiritual warfare, let's focus on Satan's only weapon and on our response to his actions. Standing, or spiritual warfare is not reserved for the saint of God who has been walking with God for 20 years. No, it is for every child of God; and God makes it possible for all of us to perform warfare in His might and power. We do not have to be experts. Remember, God gives grace to the humble. James 4:6 says, "But He gives more grace. Therefore He says, God resists the proud, but He gives grace to the humble."

There is a process that God has in transferring His will to earth.

To convert our problems into blessings takes time and it takes our patience to hang on after all hope seems to be gone.

In Luke 19:11-13 His disciples thought that the Kingdom of God was coming to earth right now, that all their problems would be solved the next day. He taught His disciples a lesson for you and me.

"And as they heard these things, he added and spake a parable, because he was nigh to Jerusalem, and because they thought that the kingdom of God should immediately appear. He said therefore, A certain nobleman went into a far country to receive for himself a kingdom, and to return. And he called his ten servants, and delivered them ten pounds, and said unto them, *Occupy* till I come" (Luke 19:11-13).

He told a parable about a king going into a distant country to obtain a kingdom and he would soon return. He called his servants and gave them each an amount of currency equal to about 4 months of salary (10 minas). He told them to *occupy* until He came back. Many of them detested his authority.

There were four classes of people present at his return.

1. The group that detested his authority and did not want anyone to reign over them were banished from his presence and killed.

2-3. Others occupied or did business and traded with the currency. According to their success, they were given more currency and rewarded with kingdom authority over many cities.

4. Others did not occupy because they thought that the king was a mean person who would punish them for *occupying*. Not only did they not get any rewards but also his currency was taken away. Use it or lose it!

What is this word *occupy*? The word *occupy* means to do business, to trade for profit. Business by definition is to take a raw material or service, add value to it and make it more profitable so it can be useful or sold. It means to exchange or to even change something to make it more profitable. It is used in the Bible to describe people who had businesses, cattle farms and other businesses both good and bad.

Proverbs 3:13-18 says, "Blessed is the man who finds wisdom, and the man who gets understanding. For the profit (merchandise, or *occupy*) from it is better than the gain from silver, and its produce more than fine gold; she is more precious than rubies; and all the things you can desire are not to be compared with her."

We are to change our problems into profit. We are to take the raw materials of problems and do business with them by producing blessings. Another word is reconcile, which means to turn something from an enemy to a friend.

The currency that this king gave to his servants was his own property. I believe that His property is His resurrection power that He gave to us through the Holy Spirit. Jesus does not have any bad things to give to us, however we do have unresolved issues to which He wants the power of His cross applied. I submit, that this is what He gives to us. We can see the afflictions as coming from the enemy, and in many ways they did, but Jesus wants us to see them as having been filtered through Him as unresolved issues. We allow His resurrection power change our enemies to friends, our junk to jewels, our curses to blessings.

Colossians 1:20 confirms this, as it says, "and by Him to reconcile [makes friends with] *all things* to Himself, by Him, whether things on earth or things in heaven, having made peace through the blood of His cross."

Matthew 25 unfolds this mystery.

The parable of the Talents. Matthew 25:14 is almost the same parable as Luke 19. The master left, and left the currency later to return.

The Wise and Foolish Virgins: Matthew 25:1 tells about 5 foolish and 5 wise virgins. The only difference was that the foolish did not hang on long enough when their bridegroom was late in keeping his promise. The foolish did not have enough oil to hang on long enough.

Virgins mean that they kept their sins cleansed before the Lord. So they were all believers. The difference is in being wise or foolish. The wisdom is hearing God speak. The Lamp would be the Word of God

(Psalm 119 & Proverb 6:23) and the oil would be the Holy Spirit. When those are combined it equals perseverance, patience, staying power and the fruit of the Spirit. Then they know that their Lord is going to come to deliver them even if all human hope is gone. They are going to hang on to what Jesus said to them no matter what. The Lord will come back now, into your situation to change your problems into blessings. The wise virgins knew their master's personality. I can hear them saying, "I don't care if he is late, he is a man of honor and integrity, he will keep his word. He will never leave me nor forsake me." The wise virgins stay connected to God and His Word and His Holy Spirit to such a degree that nothing can move them.

So what is this wisdom?

Wisdom is knowing and relying on the fact that the Cross of Jesus absorbed all the evil and everything must turn out to be a blessing. The law of gravity says that whatever goes up *must* come down. The law of the Spirit of Life in Christ Jesus (Romans 8:1) says that all evil has been disarmed, and now must be a blessing, IF you believe. It also says that there is now no condemnation if you are walking in the Spirit, as we have described.

Wisdom is knowing that all things have been reconciled through the Cross. Not just people, but all things. "And through Him having made peace through the blood of His cross, it pleased the Father to reconcile all things to Himself through Him, whether the things on earth or the things in Heaven." (Colossians 1:20)

Reconcile is a powerful word. Strong's Concordance (2) calls it "to bring back a former state of harmony." It is defined "to repair, to put back into working order, making peace between two opposing views or groups." Vines Bible Dictionary [3] defines it "to change from enmity to friendship." The Cross of Jesus Christ takes all of our "enemies," whether they be people, demons, circumstances, sickness, poverty, everything, and changes them into a friend. This is Wisdom! Christ crucified!

2 Corinthians 5:18 says, "All this is from God, who reconciled us to himself through Christ and gave us the ministry of reconciliation:" So this is our ministry here on earth, to take all the enemies of our lives, dip them into the blood and Cross of Jesus Christ, and turn them into friends. I can tell you by the Word of God and by my own experience, that this is true, it works, if you stand.

Wisdom is knowing that the blood of Jesus has defeated Satan. What does it mean to have victory over Satan? How does the blood of Jesus give us power? "Since the children have flesh and blood, he too shared in their humanity so that by his death he might destroy him who holds the power of death--that is, the devil-- and free those who all their lives were held in slavery by their fear of death" (Hebrews 2:14,15).

"Now if we died with Christ, we believe that we will also live with him. For we know that since Christ was raised from the dead, he cannot die again; death no longer has mastery over him" (Romans 6:8,9).

These verses say that Satan was "destroyed." What does that actually mean? He seems to be running around doing a job of destroying others.

The word destroy is defined in Strong's Concordance (2) as:

1) to render idle, unemployed, inactivate, inoperative.

1a) to cause a person or thing to have no further efficiency.

1b) to deprive of force, influence, power.

When Jesus and you and I were raised from the dead, we were born again as new race that is no longer subject to Satan. He has no more dominion over us. We have dominion over him. Satan used his ultimate power on Jesus at the Cross, and Jesus was resurrected after that. Satan has no more power to exert. He is out of tools and weapons.

He can still destroy an unbeliever, and he can deceive a believer, but if we know the truth, he cannot harm us any longer. As far as we are concerned, he is destroyed. If we stand on the truth, all Satan can do is lie to us. Satan has no power over the new creation; that includes you and me!

"And he is the head of the body, the church; he is the beginning and the firstborn from among the dead, so that in everything he might have the supremacy" (Colossians 1:18).

Job chapter 28 indicates that true wisdom is really found in suffering. Job 28:12 says, "But where shall wisdom be found? and where *is* the place of understanding?" The answer, I believe, indicates that when our flesh dies, when we are going through dark places of "death," then we can hear true wisdom. Job 28:22 says, "The place of ruin and death say, We have heard the fame of it with our ears." Proverbs 11:2 also supports this when it says, "When pride cometh, then cometh shame: but with the lowly is wisdom."

This is the script of life. We need to recognize where we are in it. It will make suffering more compatible. Yes, Jesus is returning to earth someday, but He will also return for you now, to turn your problem into a blessing.

A good example of this kind of overcoming is Daniel in the lion's den in Daniel chapter 6. Daniel was wholly following God and became persecuted by his enemies and God's enemies. Rather than being delivered *from* the lion's den, he overcame *in* the lion's den. The result was his enemies were totally defeated.

"At the king's command, the men who had falsely accused Daniel were brought in and thrown into the lions' den, along with their wives and children. And before they reached the floor of the den, the lions overpowered them and crushed all their bones. Then King Darius wrote to all the peoples, nations and men of every language throughout the land: 'May you prosper greatly! I issue a decree that in every part of my kingdom people must fear and reverence the God of Daniel. For he is the living God and he endures for ever; his kingdom will not be destroyed, his dominion will never end. He rescues and he saves; he performs signs and wonders in the heavens and on the earth. He has rescued Daniel from the power of the lions.' So Daniel prospered during the reign of Darius and the reign of Cyrus the Persian" (Daniel 6:24-28).

I doubt that Daniel would have prospered, and that his enemies would have been defeated if he had not gone through the lion's den.

What is our responsibility during the waiting period?

Standing requires that we do something, we are not to just wait around. Hebrews 6:12 says, " We do not want you to become lazy, but to imitate those who through faith and patience inherit what has been promised."

We must maintain our "virginity." That is we must stay clean before the Lord. We must keep short accounts with our sins, and keep them confessed and cleansed before God and man..

I also believe that the Bible teaches us that during this waiting period, we are to use the Word of God as a sword. Ephesians 6:17b says, "the sword of the Spirit, which is the word of God."

We are told in Hebrews 3:1 "Wherefore, holy brethren, partakers of the heavenly calling, consider the Apostle and High Priest of our profession, Christ Jesus." Jesus takes our confession to the Father as our High Priest, and the Father sees to it that it is accomplished, provided it is the Word of God. The enemy also takes our confession, our negative confession, and accomplishes what we say.

When the Word of God is confessed and prayed over a person or a situation, it is powerful! Jesus created everything by His Word. Jesus IS the Word. Jesus gave us the authority to use the Word as if it were He saying it!

John 1:1-3 says, "In the beginning was the Word, and the Word was with God, and the Word was God, He was in the beginning with God. All things came into being through Him, and without Him not even one thing came into being that has come into being."

When the Passover was administered to Israel in Exodus 12, the Israelites were told to put the blood of an innocent lamb over their doors and the death angel (demon) would "pass over" and not hurt them. Jesus is the Lamb of God, and we can put His blood over our doors and over the doors of our loved ones and those that we pray for. How?

Revelation 12:11 says, "And they overcame him because of the blood of the Lamb, and because of the word of their testimony. And they did not love their soul to the death."

The words of our mouth will apply the blood. Notice in Exodus 12 that as long as the lamb's blood stayed in the basin, it did no good. But when they took the hyssop, dipped it in the blood, and applied it to their door, then God and the devil could see it. The hyssop was a common weed that did not seem to have much value. The words of our mouth do not seem to have much value, but when we dip them into the Word of God (Who is Jesus Himself) and apply them as blood, God sees it and the devil sees it!

Jesus takes our confession and makes it powerful. Hebrews 3:1 says, "Therefore, holy brothers, called to be partakers of the heavenly calling, consider the Apostle and High Priest of our profession, Christ Jesus."

When we speak God's Word, Jesus takes it to the Father and asks Him to perform it.

John 16:23 says, "And in that day you shall ask Me nothing. Truly, truly, I say to you, Whatever you shall ask the Father in My name, He will give you."

Then we can enter into rest and let the Word do the work. Hebrews 4:1 says, "Therefore, a promise being left to enter into His rest, let us fear lest any of you should seem to come short of it."

Hebrews 4:12 says, "For the word of God is living and powerful and sharper than any two-edged sword, piercing even to the dividing apart of soul and spirit, and of the joints and marrow, and is a discerner of the thoughts and intents of the heart."

Angels go to work when they hear God's Word. Psalms 103:20 says, "Bless the LORD, O angels of His, who excel in strength, who do His command, listening to the voice of His word."

Demons flee! Psalms 149:5-9 says, "Let the saints be joyful in glory; let them sing aloud on their beds. Let the high praises of God be in their mouth, and a two-edged sword in their hand, to carry out vengeance on the nations and punishments on the peoples, (representing our spiritual enemies) to bind their kings with chains and their nobles with iron-bands, to carry out on them the judgment written; this is an honor for all His saints. Praise the LORD!"

Really, this is not even fair to Satan. Look how God treats him.

Luke 10:19 says, "I have given you authority to trample on snakes and scorpions and to overcome all the power of the enemy; nothing will harm you."

The enemy lost before the war started. Joshua 11:18-20 says, "Joshua waged war against all these kings for a long time. Except for the Hivites living in Gibeon, not one city made a treaty of peace with the Israelites, who took them all in battle. For it was the LORD himself who hardened their (the enemy's) hearts to wage war against Israel, so that he might destroy them totally, exterminating them (the enemy) without mercy, as the LORD had commanded Moses."

Go ahead and think of your worst problem. Now think of or look up a promise in God's Word. Now you decide. Which one is changeable, and which one is unchangeable.

"May the peoples praise you, O God; may all the peoples praise you. Then the land will yield its harvest, and God, our God, will bless us" (Psalms 67:5,6).

Section 2
Seminar 2

Blood and Fire !

Now that you have a good start, you will need the power to finish the race.

Chapters 8-11 deal with:

8.   Introduction.

9.   The Cross.

10.   Deliverance.

11.   Baptism in the Holy Spirit.

Chapter 8
Power to Run the Race - Introduction

In the first Section of this book, the first 7 chapters, we learned that there is hope for those of us who cannot find hope in the "world system." We found that we can repent (turn) from depending upon the world, and the Kingdom of God will be at hand (within our reach).

We learned that Jesus taught in Mark 4:11 that the mystery of the Kingdom of God was contained in the parable of the sower. He taught that the Word of God is the seed, our hearts are the ground, and the result will be fruit.

The fruit would change our character into the character of Jesus, it would supply our personal needs and it would thrust us out into a dying world to bear the fruit of eternal life for others.

We learned about the many steps in the process of the seed becoming actual fruit.

Here is the theme of Grow or Die:

1) We need to turn to the Kingdom of God, the Word, for fruit.

2) We need to know how to be intimate with God - which is The Flowing River.

3) We need to know how to get out and stay out of being Prisoners in the Promise Land.

4) We need to know more about God's character - Who God is.

5) We need to know our true identity in Jesus - SIT.

6) We need to take up our cross and walk in obedience to the Word - WALK.

7) We learned in the STAND lesson that there is a spiritual enemy that is opposed to this entire process, Satan and his company of devils and demons. We learned that we need patience and staying power to stand until the fruit comes forth. Another way to put it is, we need to wait for the Lord to come to fulfill the promise. "We do not want you to become lazy, but to imitate those who through faith and patience inherit what has been promised" (Hebrews 6:12).

I thank God if you have embraced this process given to us by the Word of God. If you have, you will need power in your life to complete the process and to see the manifestation of fruit in your life.

Just as plants need water and fertilizer for power until they bear fruit, we also need power. Section 2 is dedicated to helping you understand how to appropriate this power.

Our life in Christ is not an experience, but a race.

It is good to start a race, but we need to know how to finish. Many people start and never finish. We need the power to finish the race otherwise we will lose. Hebrews 12:1 says, "Therefore since we also are surrounded with so great a cloud of witnesses, let us lay aside every weight and the sin which so easily besets us, and let us run with patience the race that is set before us."

The Scriptures tell us that the power we need is found in:
1. The Cross or the blood of Jesus. "For the message of the cross is foolishness to those who are perishing, but to us who are being saved it is the **power** of God" (1 Corinthians 1:18).
2. The delivering power of God. "And as he was yet a coming, the devil threw him down, and tare *him*. And Jesus rebuked the unclean spirit, and healed the child, and delivered him again to his father. And they were all amazed at the mighty **power** of God" (Luke 9:42,43a).
3. The fullness of the Holy Spirit. "But you will receive power when the Holy Spirit comes on you; and you will be my witnesses in Jerusalem, and in all Judea and Samaria, and to the ends of the earth" (Acts 1:8).

God did not leave us orphans here on earth to provide for ourselves until we die and go to Heaven. He is very practical. He has a method of taking care of us in the here and now, but many have been ignorant of His method. "I will not leave you as orphans [fatherless]; I will come to you" (John 14:18). Jesus was talking about the coming of the Holy Spirit. In the following chapters we will discuss how the Holy Spirit is vital in keeping us from being orphans, fatherless and without help in this world.

The Cross of Jesus is what defeated Satan and gave us victory. That is power. The truth of the Cross acted on by us gives us power. I submit however, that the truth of the Cross cannot be fully appropriated in our lives without the power spoken of in Acts 1:8, the fullness of the Holy Spirit.

For example, the power to operate lights in a building originates in the generator that is creating the electricity. You could stand there and look at the electric outlet in the wall and admire it and know that it has power in it, but until you plug the light into the socket you have not appropriated the power for yourself.

We are going to find out about the truth of the power of the Cross, and we are going to find out how to make it personal in your life.

Chapter 9
The Cross

Let us first focus on the Cross and the blood of Jesus.

Christians have spoken about the Cross of Jesus Christ for thousands of years, yet so very few really comprehend its full meaning and how it relates to their lives. Many people have heard about the blood of Jesus, but have not fully understood its value and true meaning.

In John chapter 6, Jesus saw the multitudes of poor people, and with compassion He fed them with a miracle of loaves and fishes. This was great for the people. So great that they decided to follow Jesus all the way to the other side of the lake so that they could eat again with another miracle.

Jesus refused to perform the same miracle the next day. He told the people that He had a permanent cure for their poverty. He indicated that they needed to get rid of their poverty through a blood covenant. They needed to eat His flesh and drink His blood. Many became offended, thinking that He was asking them to actually become a cannibal and eat His physical body. He then told them that they would be even more offended if He left and they could not find Him to eat of Him.

Then He made the transition to the spiritual He said, "The Spirit gives life; the flesh counts for nothing. The words I have spoken to you are spirit and they are life" (John 6:63). He was saying that if you want to partake of the blood and the life of God, you must do it through His Word. Read the story in John 6.

Our deliverance from every kind of "poverty" in life is provided for in the blood covenant with God. The Cross and the blood of Jesus represent the blood covenant.

Satan is out to trick us and blind us to the real power of the Cross.

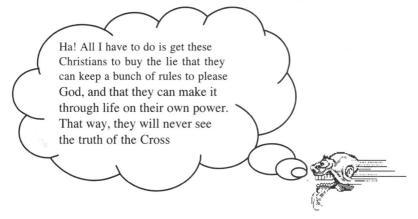

Ha! All I have to do is get these Christians to buy the lie that they can keep a bunch of rules to please God, and that they can make it through life on their own power. That way, they will never see the truth of the Cross

Satan tries very hard to hide the true message of the Cross.
Galatians 3:1-3a says, "You foolish Galatians! Who has bewitched you?
Before your very eyes Jesus Christ was clearly portrayed as crucified."

Galatians 3:10 says, "All who rely on observing the Law are under a
curse, for it is written: 'Cursed is everyone who does not continue to do
everything written in the Book of The Law.'"

Paul was telling these Galatian believers that they had been bewitched
by Satan into ignoring the Cross and paying attention to two things:

1. Legalism. Living by rules and not by a relationship with Jesus.
2. The power of their flesh or old nature. Trying to do it in their own
power.

Witchcraft is the power that attempts to manipulate and control you and
puts you under the wrong authority. It always controls and manipulates. In
this case, the Galatians were put under the authority of a demon who had
convinced them that their own soulish nature (the flesh) and legalism were
the way to please God. This was obscuring the real Gospel and the power
of the Cross.

If you were Satan, and Jesus had totally defeated you at the Cross, and
you knew that God's people could be tricked into not knowing about your
defeat and their victory, what would you do?

Would you spread a lie that says, "You need to keep all these laws to
be right with God, and you have it in you to perform everything that God
requires. You don't need to know about the power of the Cross and the
Blood of Jesus. That is just a bunch of religious tradition?" That is the
same lie that the Rich Young Ruler was bewitched with in Matthew 19.
Look it up and read it.

Paul was so upset with this teaching that he said something very radical
in Galatians 1:8 which is, "But even if we or an angel from Heaven preach a
gospel to you beside what we preached to you, let him be accursed."

The Apostle Paul preached only the Cross. According to Galatians
6:14-15, Paul indicated that keeping the laws was not something to be
preached. Instead, Paul preached the Cross, which resulted in the new birth.

Satan spends his energy keeping us from the truth of the Cross
because it represents a blood covenant between God and man.

The Cross is what defeated Satan.
We are going to focus on two aspects of a blood covenant:
1. The law of exchange.

2. Intimacy.

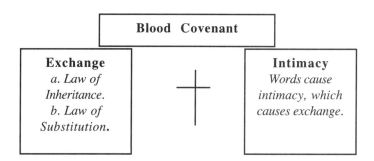

1. First, we will discuss the Law of Exchange. This has two parts, the Law of Inheritance and the Law of Substitution.

God set up some laws before the foundation of the world that are the basis for the law of exchange. They both operate by blood. They both make up the law of exchange.

1. The Law of Exchange in a blood covenant. We will present the two parts.

First here is Part 1-A The Law of Inheritance.

We inherit blessings and curses from our family going back many generations.

God set up the human race where the life is in the blood. Leviticus 17:11 says, "For the life of the flesh is in the blood. And I have given it to you on the altar to make an atonement for your souls. For it is the blood that makes an atonement for the soul." John 6:56 says, "He that eats my flesh and drinks my blood dwells in me and I in him."

We inherit blessings and curses from our forefathers. Exodus 34:6-8 says, "And The Lord passed by before his (Moses') face and called out: The Lord! The Lord God! Merciful and gracious, slow to anger, and great in goodness and truth, keeping mercy for thousands, forgiving iniquity and transgression and sin, and not leaving entirely unpunished, visiting the iniquity of fathers on sons, and on sons of sons, to the third and to the fourth generation. And Moses hurried and bowed to the earth and worshipped." This statement seems like a paradox. How can God forgive and still not leave unpunished?

We create blessings and curses with our own sin. Romans 6:23 says, "For the wages of sin is death, but the gift of God is eternal life through Jesus Christ our Lord." Galatians 7:7 says, "Do not be deceived, God is not mocked. For whatever a man sows, that he also will reap."

Where does the law of inheritance live? Is it in the body or the spirit? Both. That is why people look like their parents. The invisible part of what is inherited in the spirit fools most people. There are two parts of a person that can have life or family inheritance.

John 3:5-6 says, "Jesus answered, Truly, truly, I say to you, Unless a man is born of water and the Spirit, he cannot enter into the kingdom of God. That which is born of the flesh is flesh, and that which is born of the Spirit is spirit."

The physical life. The physical life carries the looks and build of the body.

The spiritual life. The spiritual life is the life that carries the inheritance of blessings and curses.

That does not seem fair, but there is a solution.
This is the Good News!

Part 1-B The Law of Substitution.

Example. The law of gravity keeps an airplane on the ground. But when the airplane taxies down the runway fast enough another law takes over and nullifies the law of gravity; that is the law of lift. In the same way, the law of substitution nullifies the law of inheritance.

This law means that people may be born into a certain family and from that family lineage they will receive blessings and curses as their inheritance, but the curses can be changed. Tribes in Africa, in American Indian culture and some Asian societies have always looked for ways to swap or trade blessings and curses with other people. They would trade weapons, coats, and other important articles as a sign that they were committed to each other and would protect one another to the death. In some African cultures, if a family adopted a child, the father would shed blood and put it on the hands of the child to make the child his own.

Since ancient times, people have drank blood that was offered to their god, so that they could be like God.

94

Before the foundation of the world, God prearranged to have Jesus crucified according to the eternal Spirit, which means that the substitution principle was in effect before any man was created. Revelation 13:8b says, ".... in the Book of Life of the Lamb having been slain from the foundation of the world."

A good example of the law of substitution was the Passover. Exodus 12:13-14 says, "And the blood shall be a sign to you upon the houses where you are. And when I see the blood, I will pass over you. And the plague shall not be upon you for destruction when I smite in the land of Egypt. And this day shall be a memorial to you. And you shall keep it as a feast to the LORD throughout your generations. You shall keep it as a feast by a law forever." The life of the lamb, represented by its blood, was the substitute for the first born in the family. The lamb died instead of the first born child. The Passover lamb needed to be without blemish, it had to be perfect.

This is the reason Jesus needed to be born of a virgin, unspotted by the sin of the Adamic race. The only way He could be our Passover Lamb was to be unspotted and perfect. His Father was God, his mother was Mary. He is all God and all man. He is the second Adam, without sin, and capable of taking our sin.

This explains the paradox (on the previous page) in Exodus 34:6-8. The only way God could extend mercy to humans and still not leave their sin unpunished would be to punish Jesus, the perfect Lamb of God in their place.

God foretold that the law of substitution would take place in the new covenant. Jeremiah 31:29-34 says, "In those days they shall not say any more, The fathers have eaten sour grapes, and the teeth of the sons are dull. But every man shall die in his iniquity. Every man who eats the sour grapes, his teeth will be dull. Behold, the days come, says the LORD, that I will cut a new covenant with the house of Israel, and with the house of Judah, not according to the covenant that I cut with their fathers in the day I took them by the hand to bring them out of the land of Egypt; which covenant of Mine they broke, although I was a husband to them, says the LORD; but this shall be the covenant that I will cut with the house of Israel: After those days, says the LORD, I will put My law in their inward parts, and write it in their hearts; and I will be their God, and they shall be My people. And they shall no more teach each man his neighbor and each man his brother, saying, Know the LORD; for they shall all know me, from the least of them to the greatest of them, says the LORD. For I will forgive their iniquity, and I will remember their sins no more."

The law of substitution can exchange the spiritual life. A blood covenant changes your family inheritance.

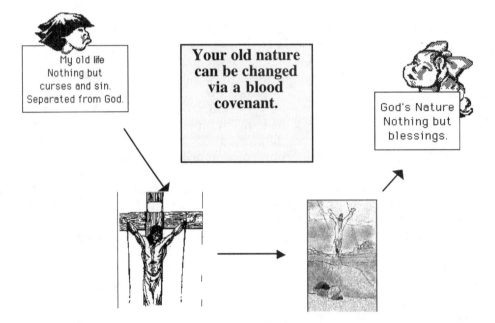

My old life
Nothing but
curses and sin.
Separated from God.

Your old nature can be changed via a blood covenant.

God's Nature
Nothing but
blessings.

Galatians 2:20 says, "I have been crucified with Christ, and I live; yet no longer I, but Christ lives in me. And that life I now live in the flesh, I live by faith toward the Son of God, who loved me and gave Himself on my behalf."

Isaiah 53:4-12 says, "Surely He has borne our griefs, and carried our sorrows; yet we esteemed Him stricken, smitten of God, and afflicted. But He was wounded for our transgressions; He was bruised for our iniquities; the chastisement of our peace was on Him; and with His stripes we ourselves are healed. All we like sheep have gone astray; we have turned, each one to his own way; and the LORD has laid on Him the iniquity of us all."

People for ages have endeavored to change their spiritual life by changing physical blood.

Many cultures still make blood covenants. However, this does not really work because they are just dealing with the physical life. They may be committed to each other, but nothing inside them has really changed; their spirit is still the same. Hebrews 9:13-14 says, "The blood of goats and bulls and the ashes of a heifer sprinkled on those who are ceremonially unclean sanctify them so that they are outwardly clean. How much more, then, will the blood of Christ, who through the eternal Spirit offered himself unblemished to God, cleanse our consciences from acts that lead to death, so that we may serve the living God!" There are many counterfeits used by primitive cultures and occults.

What does the Cross or the blood covenant exchange for us? What did it give us, what did it give Jesus?

First, it gave Jesus everything we are. He died a criminal's death because we were rebels.

We were all rebels and criminals before God redeemed us. Adam and Eve's sin was rebellion (i.e. not obeying God's voice and Word). We were born into rebellion or sin.

Ephesians 2:1-6 says, "And He has made you alive, who were once dead in trespasses and sins, in which you once walked according to the course of this world, according to the prince of the power of the air, the spirit that now works in the children of disobedience; among whom we also had our way of life in times past, in the lusts of our flesh, fulfilling the desires of the flesh and of the thoughts, and were by nature the children of wrath, even as others. But God, who is rich in mercy, for His great love with which He loved us (even when we were dead in sins) has made us alive together with Christ (by grace you are saved), and has raised us up together and made us sit together in the heavenlies in Christ Jesus."

The Story about Barabbas. Matthew 27:16 says that Barabbas was a notorious prisoner. There were three crosses on Golgotha. The two on either side were made for criminals. Who was the middle cross made for, Jesus? No, It was made for Barabbas. Jesus took his place. Isaiah 53 says that Jesus took our place.

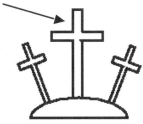

Isaiah 53:4-6 says, "Surely He has borne our griefs, and carried our sorrows; yet we esteemed Him stricken, smitten of God, and afflicted. But He was wounded for our transgressions; He was bruised for our iniquities; the chastisement of our peace was on Him; and with His stripes we ourselves are healed. All we like sheep have gone astray; we have turned, each one to his own way; and the LORD has laid on Him the iniquity of us all."

Second, it gave us everything God is and God has.

Listed here are some of the major exchanges Jesus made for us that we may enjoy. (Check out the opposites!) Some of these are weights, some are sins. A weight is something that is oppressing you, a burden, most likely imposed upon you by another (Hebrews 12:1). (Many of these examples were taken from the teachings of Derek Prince.)

1. Jesus was **punished** that we might be **forgiven** (Isaiah 53: 4-5, Ephesians 4:32, Colossians 2:13).

2. Jesus was **wounded** that we might be **healed** (Isaiah 53:4-5, Matthew 8:16-17, 1 Peter 2:24).

3. Jesus was **made sin** with our sinfulness that we might be **made righteous** with His righteousness (Isaiah 53:10, 2 Corinthians 5:21). **Righteousness** means to be in good standing with God (Romans 3:22, Romans 4:6, Romans 10:10).

4. Jesus died our **death** that we might share His **life**. The wages of sin is death (Romans 6:23, Hebrews 2:9, John 8:52).

5. Jesus was made a **curse** that we might receive the **blessing** (Galatians 3:13-14, Deuteronomy 21:22-23, Deuteronomy 28:1-13).

Some curses:
Mental and emotional breakdowns.
Repeated or chronic sickness and disease - especially hereditary.
Repeated miscarriage or female problems.
Breakdown of marriage and family- marriage to wrong partners.
Continued financial insufficiency, especially when income appears to be sufficient.
Accident-prone.
Suicides or unnatural deaths.
Addictions, such as alcohol and drugs.
Rebellion to authority.
Unnatural sexual tendencies.
Appropriating the power of the Cross will deliver you from these and many more curses. Get ready!

6. Jesus endured our **poverty** that we might share His **abundance** (2 Corinthians 8:9 and 9:8).
Sufficiency is just enough; abundance is more than enough so that we can bless others. Jesus was hungry, thirsty, naked and in need at the Cross.

7. Jesus bore our **shame** that we might share His **glory** (Matthew 27:35-36).
Hebrews 2:10 says that Jesus brings many sons to glory (not shame).
We can receive the fullness of the Holy Spirit. The Holy Spirit counteracts shame.
Sexual abuse causes shame.
We obtain the slavery mindset through shame.
We get self-esteem problems through shame.

8. Jesus endured our **rejection** that we might have His **acceptance** with the Father (Matthew 27:45-51). The Father hid His face from Jesus and rejected Him for us. Ephesians 1:6 says we are accepted by the Father.

People are hungry to be accepted, to feel as if they belong, as if they matter to someone. Only Jesus can give this. His Church is the place for belonging. Children need their father's acceptance. Love must be openly expressed. Divorce causes rejection (Isaiah 54:6). Jesus died of a broken heart. "Accept one another, then, just as Christ accepted you, in order to bring praise to God" (Romans 15:7). God accepts us in our sinful condition (Ephesians 1:3-6).

9. Jesus was **cut off from the Father** by death that we might enjoy **God's presence** eternally (Matthew 27:46, Isaiah 53:8, Hebrews

10:21-22, Jude 24, Colossians 1:27, Ephesians 3:16-20). Our need for emotional security is satisfied. The fullness of the Holy Spirit is available to give us God's presence (Acts 1:8).

10. Our "old man" (sin nature) was put to **death** in Him, that the new man (Christ's nature) might come to **life** in us (Romans 6:6, Galatians 2:20).
Forgiveness of sins is great, but doing away with the person that sins is greater.

11. Jesus experienced our **sorrows** and bore our **griefs** that we might have **gladness and joy** (Isaiah 53, Isaiah 35:10, Isaiah 51:11).
Death of a loved one, loss of some kind, pending disaster, overwhelming worry and sadness can cause hopelessness in your life, even a potential for suicide. The Holy Spirit brings us joy.

12. Jesus kept the **law** for us so that we could live by **grace** (Romans 7:6 and 8:1-4, Ephesians 2:8-9, Galatians 3:1-3).
Living by legalism is promoting the power of the flesh (1 Corinthians 15:56). It leads to frustration, failure, addictions, condemnation, and backsliding.

13. Jesus was **tormented** that we might enjoy **peace** (Isaiah 53:5, Philippians 4:7).

14. Jesus was made **insignificant** that we might have **significance**. He was sold for the price of a slave (Matthew 26:15, 1 Peter 1:18-19). The price God paid for us makes us significant.

15. Jesus was **captured** by the world, so that we could be **delivered** from the world, this present evil age (Galatians 1:4 and 6:14). The world has been crucified to us and we have been crucified to the world.

16. **Evil was conquered.** Jesus (appeared to have) suffered **defeat by evil** that we might **enjoy victory over evil**.

The Cross Was Absolute.
It disarmed and defeated Satan and every evil that ever existed, even the evil that looks as if it is coming on you. No matter what hits you, it must turn into a blessing. Colossians 2:14-15 says, "[Jesus] blotting out the handwriting of ordinances that was against us, [all the right that Satan had to do evil to us] which was contrary to us, and has taken it out of the way, nailing it to the **cross**. Having stripped rulers and authorities [demons and

Satan], He made a show of them publicly, triumphing over them in it." See *also Mark 16:15-19 and Romans 6:9.*

All things have been reconciled through the Cross. Not just people, but all things. "And through Him having made peace through the blood of His cross, it pleased the Father to reconcile all things to Himself through Him, whether the things on earth or the things in Heaven" (Colossians 1:20).

"Reconcile" is a powerful word. Strong's Concordance (2) defines it "to bring back a former state of harmony." It is defined "to repair, to put back into working order, making peace between two opposing views or groups."

Vines Bible Dictionary (3) defines it as "to change from enmity to friendship." The Cross of Jesus Christ takes all of our enemies, whether they be people, demons, circumstances, sickness, poverty, everything bad and changes them into a friend.

2 Corinthians 5:18 says, "All this is from God, who reconciled us to himself through Christ and gave us the ministry of reconciliation." This is our ministry here on earth; to take all the enemies of our lives, dip them into the blood and Cross of Jesus Christ, and turn them into friends. I can tell you by the Word of God and by my own experience that this is true. It works if you stand.

How can you make the benefits of the Cross real in your life? How can you have intimacy with God? You must take up YOUR cross.

The Cross of Jesus Christ will sit there without power unless we connect it with our cross. Only then will the Blood Covenant be real for us.

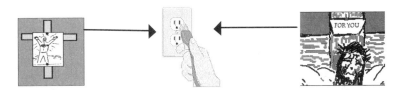

People underestimate the power of our choice.

It is the second most powerful thing in the universe, after the power of God. "And He said to all, If anyone desires to come after Me, let him deny himself and take up his cross daily and follow Me. For whoever will save his life shall lose it, but whoever will lose his life for My sake, he shall save it. For what is a man profited if he gains the whole world and loses himself, or is cast away?" (Luke 9:23-25).

101

Here is a test of your willingness to take up your cross. Mark each item yes or no.

Do not check these items without a lot of thought and commitment. These are serious life and death issues. Do not lie to God; do not lie to yourself. It is better to pass and not check these off if you do not mean it.

_____ **I am willing to be honest with my condition (weight or sin) - totally honest!**

_____ **I am tired of my weight or sin and I want to be free.**

_____ **I am tired of trying to make life work on my own. I turn to the Word of God to bear fruit, His way.**

_____ **I repent, (go the other direction) and I ask for God's help.**

_____ **I turn my back on the things of this "world."**

_____ **I believe what the Word says about Jesus taking my weight and sin.**

_____ **I make Jesus Lord (boss) and I make a decision to follow Him through His Word and Spirit.**

_____ **I exchange God's will for my will. I forgive those who hurt me.**

_____ **I exchange my mind for God's mind.**

_____ **I exchange my emotions for God's emotions.**

_____ **I am willing to experience persecution and I am not be ashamed of Jesus.**

_____ **I am willing to step out from the crowd and not care what they think of me.**

_____ **I am willing to be faithful with what is in my hand right now.**

_____ **I will live by His Word every day and spend much time in it.**

____ I will continue to believe by continuing with Jesus and the Word as my Lord. I will make it a priority to take time to build a relationship with God.

____ I will stand against all the lies of the devil, no matter how long it takes.

____ I will step out from the crowd and become lost in God.

____ I will drop my pride about what others think and ask God to give me all He has.

____ I will spend quality fellowship time with Jesus daily. I will pour out my heart to Him in total honesty.

Receive now.

 Let's exchange some things right now!

Instructions:

IF you marked **YES** to all of the above, then proceed. If you did not answer YES, then you should ask God to change your heart. He can do that.

1. Then turn back to the exchange section where the 16 exchanges are listed. Circle the "light bulbs" that apply to you.
2. Look up the Scriptures and confess them with your mouth.
3. Write them on a piece of paper and read them out loud daily.

Now thank Jesus for what He has done for YOU.

2. Now we will deal with intimacy in a blood covenant.

I believe that a majority of people do not truly understand intimacy. God created every person with the desire for intimacy. We all crave it, but we do not understand the proper way to pursue it and express it. People have perverted intimacy in many ways.

Most people, when they think of intimacy, think of sex. Sex is only a small part (and the result) of some types of intimacy, it is not the main factor however.

Intimacy as a child. Doctors have discovered that if babies do not have intimacy, they will die. Even as children we are designed to have intimacy with our parents. It is something that is required; it is God's design. So many parents bruise their children for life by not giving them intimacy. They teach them that hugging and crying is not proper. They teach them to bury their needs, not knowing that their needs will appear in a perverted form. All of us need the affirmation of a father. Most addictions can be traced to a broken relationship with the father.

Intimacy with spouses. So often we gain intimacy with our future spouse while we are courting, but after marriage many treat them like slaves. We should rather continue and even increase our intimacy and romance.

Intimacy with God. God wants intimacy with us. He gave us the Song of Songs or Song of Solomon as His example of this. Look at verses 2:14, 7:13, and 8:6-7. Luke 10:39 tells about Mary who spent time at the feet of Jesus, listening to His Word. Jesus thought this was extremely valuable!

Intimacy is originated through words, eye contact and through time spent with one another.

Exclusiveness is one key element of intimacy. Both parties need to know that there are no others involved. They need to know that they are exclusive and that the other party is devoted only to them. Some call it a single eye. The marriage relationship is likened to our intimate relationship with the Lord.

Intimacy requires taking time to talk and to listen. There is a desire to spend time with the other person. Take as an example the woman with the alabaster box in Mark 14:3. Jesus thought that this kind of "waste" was not waste at all. He said that it was part of the Gospel and that the Gospel should produce this action.

Intimacy requires stepping out from the crowd. It requires becoming lost in another person. The Rich Young Ruler in Matthew 19 did not really want intimacy with God, he was only interested in religion. He wanted his other possessions more than a relationship with God. Look at the contrast with blind Bartimaeus in Mark 10:46. He also had something to trust in. However he gave up his beggar's robe that he trusted in and cast himself completely upon Jesus.

Moses wanted intimacy with God. Moses, at the burning bush, got a taste of God's presence. Later in Exodus 33 he begged God to let him see

His glory again. He wanted to see God's glory at any cost. We need to become lost in the Lord and be dead in Christ, to no longer care about ourselves or what others think.

Psalm 91 describes the Secret Place of the Most High. Song of Solomon 2:14 talks about the same secret place as a place of intimacy where the two people see each other's faces and hear each other's voices.

The 120 people in Acts chapter 2 devoted themselves, wasted themselves in and for His presence.

"Yada" is a strong word for intimacy. Genesis 4:1 says that Adam knew Eve and she conceived. The word knew is yada, a Hebrew word that means knowing at a level of intimacy. It is used again in Proverbs 3:4-5 when it tells us to acknowledge Him in all our ways and He will direct our paths. The word acknowledge comes from yada. Jesus said in John 17:3 that eternal life is knowing (yada) Him and the Father.

Intimacy with God and your spouse should lead to oneness, the two actually change and become one. Jesus changed and became sin for us, we can change and become one with Him.

We need to step out from the crowd. Take up your cross to denominations, friends, family, customs and pride. Worship God in humility, and with reverence, bowing down before Him.

In the Flowing River lesson we took up our cross for moral sins, for our will and our intellect. This is going deeper in all three areas. It is bearing the shame of the Cross, becoming lost in God.

When God originates intimacy, our only response is worship. Holy, Holy, Holy (Revelation 4:8-11).

In 1 Samuel 1-2 Hannah risked humiliation and was indeed humiliated because she was hungry for God. She was desperate. The woman who touched the hem of His garment was humiliated, but she was desperate (Matthew 9:20).

Intimacy is God's design for the transfer of the blood covenant.

Intimacy involves the exchange of words between two parties. It involves listening to one another. Remember what Jesus told the people in John 6:63. "It is the Spirit that makes alive, the flesh profits nothing. The **words** that I speak to you are spirit and are life" (John 6:63).

We practice intimacy with God by giving Him our words and by taking in His Word. This automatically transfers more of the blood covenant to us.

We are not supposed to become cannibals and cut our wrists in order to have a blood covenant with God!

Words are the bridge of communication between the natural and the spiritual worlds. Words contain "spiritual blood."

The only way a blood covenant can be made between two beings, one being in the spiritual world and the other in the natural world, is through words.

Luke 4:4 says, "And Jesus answered him, saying, It is written that 'man shall not live by bread alone, but by every Word of God.'"

Hebrews 4:12 says, "For the Word of God is living and powerful and sharper than any two-edged sword, piercing even to the dividing apart of soul and spirit, and of the joints and marrow, and is a discerner of the thoughts and intents of the heart."

Jesus is the Word. He was and is the bridge. John 1:1-3 says, "In the beginning was the Word, and the Word was with God, and the Word was God. He was in the beginning with God. All things came into being through Him, and without Him not even one thing came into being that has come into being."

John 15:7 says, "If you live in Me, and My Words live in you, you shall ask what you will, and it shall be done to you."

John 8:51 says, "Truly, truly, I say to you, If a man keeps My Word, he shall never see death."

The Power of God is within our reach!

Romans 10:8-11 says, "But what does it say? '(The Word, is near you, even in your mouth and in your heart'; that is the Word of faith which we proclaim; Because if you confess the Lord Jesus, and believe in your heart that God has raised Him from the dead, you shall be saved. For with the heart one believes unto righteousness, and with the mouth one confesses unto salvation. For the Scripture says, 'Everyone believing on Him shall not be put to shame.'"

"For by your words you will be acquitted, and by your words you will be condemned" (Matthew 12:37).

Make time with God and give His word a priority. It will give you both intimacy and exchange!

We want things to happen fast.

God says we must have patience.

Jesus conquered all evil at the Cross, but the lie is powerful. Satan will do his best to steal what you have coming. You will win if you have patience and stand!

Warfare is required. This does not come easy!

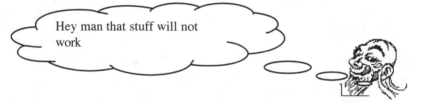

It takes time and faithfulness. Most of the time, receiving the benefits of the Cross includes a trial of time, patience and some sort of mental suffering where you feel that God is not going to come through.

James 1:2-4 says, "My brothers, count it all joy when you fall into different kinds of temptations, knowing that the trying of your faith works patience. But let patience have its perfect work, so that you may be perfect and entire, lacking nothing."

Luke 8:8 and 15 says, "And other fell on good ground and sprang up, and bore fruit a hundredfold. And when He had said these things, He cried, He who has ears to hear, let him hear. (15) But those on the good ground are the ones who, in an honest and good heart, having heard the Word, keep it and bring forth fruit with patience."

Revelation 12:11 says, "And they overcame him because of the blood of the Lamb, and because of the word of their testimony. And they did not love their soul to the death."

The waiting purifies us.

1 Peter 1:6-7 says, "You should be exceedingly glad on this account, though now for a little while you may be distressed by trials and suffer temptations, so that the genuineness of your faith may be tested, which is infinitely more precious than the perishable gold which is tested and purified by fire. This proving of your faith is intended to rebound to your praise and glory and honor when Jesus Christ the Messiah is revealed."

The Cross is absolute, but the lie is powerful. We need Wisdom.

Wisdom is knowing and relying on the fact that the Cross of Jesus absorbed all the evil and every situation must turn out to be a blessing. The law of gravity says that whatever goes up MUST come down. The law of exchange and the law of the Spirit of Life in Christ Jesus (Romans 8:1) says that all evil has been disarmed and now must be a blessing, IF you believe.

Wisdom is knowing that the blood of Jesus has defeated Satan.

"Since the children have flesh and blood, he too shared in their humanity so that by his death he might destroy him who holds the power of death--that is, the devil-- and free those who all their lives were held in slavery by their fear of death" (Hebrews 2:14,15).

We are to change our problems into profit.

We are to take the raw materials of problems and do business with them by producing blessings. Another word is reconcile, which means to turn something from an enemy to a friend (reconcile).

Waiting on God is the script of life.

We need to recognize where we are in the script. It will make suffering more compatible. Yes, Jesus is returning to Earth someday, but He will also return for you now to turn your problem into a blessing.

What is our guarantee that this will work?

The Resurrection is our guarantee. If Jesus had not been resurrected, you would have no hope. The fact that He was resurrected is conclusive evidence that your problems cannot hurt you if you are willing to be a change agent for God.

Jesus is our guarantee. What is our confidence for inheriting promises that look as if they cannot be fulfilled? He swore by Himself! Hebrews 6:15-20 indicates that God took an oath that He could not lie. Not only did He give us a promise, but also He took an oath, which in effect is saying, "I swear on my own life and with my own life that I will perform this promise. You can count on it since you ran to my Word for hope. This hope is your anchor to cling to, and is grounded in my very presence."

This is our confidence. This is how we know that the promises of God will come to pass. God swore by Himself, having no higher being to swear by. He said that if the promise did not come to pass, that He would die. He did die, through Jesus on the Cross. Jesus took our curse that we could inherit all He is and all He has. I encourage every reader to study Hebrews chapter 6 in this context .

Jesus' resurrection is our guarantee!

Here is a simple way to remember this idea without a lot of trouble

In Exodus chapter 4, Moses was not sure about his assignment that God had given to him. God told him to throw down the rod that was in his hand. When he did, it turned into a serpent. Then God told him to pick it up again and it turned back into a rod. This is the entire message in a nutshell.

The Rod is the Word. The Word is also Jesus who became sin for us on the Cross (the serpent). When Moses picked up the evil serpent, it turned back into the Word or a blessing. Jesus absorbed the evil out of the serpent and made it a blessing.

Because of the Cross of Jesus we can be sure that whatever evil we touch will turn into a blessing. Mark 16:18- and you shall pick up serpents it will not hurt you but turn you into a healer.

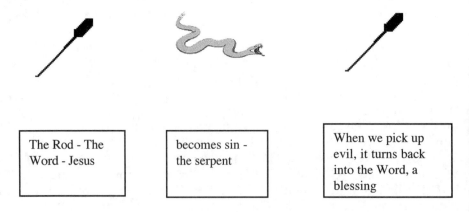

| The Rod - The Word - Jesus | becomes sin - the serpent | When we pick up evil, it turns back into the Word, a blessing |

Chapter 10
Deliverance

The Holy Spirit is the power of God for deliverance in our lives. "And as he was yet a coming, the devil threw him down, and tare *him*. And Jesus rebuked the unclean spirit, and healed the child, and delivered him again to his father. And they were all amazed at the mighty power of God" (Luke 9:42,43a).

In the New Testament, the Holy Spirit is often referred to as the Finger of God. "But if I drive out demons by the finger of God, then the Kingdom of God has come to you" (Luke 11:20). Jesus made it clear that He drove out demons by the Holy Spirit.

Our spiritual enemies often keep believers from running a successful race with God by spreading lies that they do not affect Christians. So often believers are beset with sin and weights that are put on them by devils and demons. We agree that a believer cannot be demon "possessed," but I do know that they can be demon oppressed and influenced. It does not matter where the demon resides in the believer's life, the main issue is that we need to know about them so we can get them out of our lives, wherever they are.

1. What are demons and devils, and who is Satan?

a. Satan was arch-angel Lucifer. He was in charge of worship for God. According to Ezekiel 28 and other Scriptures, he was highly anointed, and probably had built in musical instruments in his body. He was in Eden with Adam and Eve. He was beautiful. He has a very keen talent for business and merchandising. He probably created the idea of becoming wealthy with slavery. He is very proud, and realizes his own beauty. He is very intelligent and cunning. He is highly organized.

b. Lucifer rebelled against God and took 1/3 of the angels. He organized them in military order and counterfeited the Kingdom of God (Ephesians 6).

c. Satan is now the Prince of the World (John 12:31).

d. Some say demons are fallen angels, some say they are disembodied spirits perhaps from a pre-Adamic race, or perhaps even from our ancestors. The Scriptures are not conclusive on this subject. However, angels were never designed to inhabit humans. I believe that there could be both: those who were angels and who now rule with Satan, and those who are disembodied spirits who inhabit humans. I am not sure, that is purely supposition. Nevertheless, that definition is not important. The word for demon is daimon, which literally means "to know," or "the knowing one."

e. Their character is extremely filthy. <u>Vines Dictionary</u> (3) says, "demons are the spiritual agents acting in all idolatry. The idol itself is nothing, but every idol has a demon associated with it who induces idolatry, with it worship and sacrifices, 1 Co. 10:20-21; Rev. 9:20; Isa. 13:21. They disseminate errors among men, and seek to seduce believers, 1 Tim. 4:1. As seducing spirits they deceive men into the supposition that through mediums they can converse with deceased human beings. Acting under Satan, demons are permitted to afflict with bodily disease, Luke 13:16. Being unclean they tempt human beings with unclean thoughts, Matt. 10:1. They differ in degrees of wickedness, Matt. 12:45. They will instigate the rulers of the nations at the end of this age to make war against God and His Christ, Rev. 16:14."

2. What do they do? According to John 10:10 they kill, steal and destroy. Everything that they do falls under these three categories.

a. Kill. Their murder has to do with eternal damnation, and with death in this life as well.

b. Steal. They are thieves. They steal God's will for you. They steal the Word of God out of your heart. They steal virginity, health, peace, and possessions.

c. Destroy. They destroy lives. They destroy with drugs and sickness. They destroy families. They destroy with violence, sexual abuse and plagues like AIDS.

3. How do they accomplish their goals?

a. They tempt you (Matthew 4:1). The goal is to separate you from God by acting independent of God.

b. They speak to your mind (2 Corinthians 10:4).

c. They navigate circumstances (2 Thessalonians 2:9).

d. They steal the Word in order to neutralize Christians to become unfruitful (Mark 4).

e. They convince people that devils and demons do not exist. Often they use innocent looking people who appear to be nice, sometimes even Christians. I have met people in churches who were obviously influenced by demons, who have told me that demons and the entire supernatural realm is not real. They claim that evil is just something that humans do.

f. They convince you to sin so that they may have more control and Jesus less control. The wages of sin is death (Romans 6:23).

g. They lie and accuse the innocent (John 8:44 and 2 Thessalonians 2:9-10). They also accused Jesus of having demons. "For John came neither eating nor drinking, and they say, He hath a devil" (Matthew 11:18). "And the scribes which came down from Jerusalem said, He hath Beelzebub, and by the prince of the devils casteth he out devils" (Mark 3:22).

h. They take the moral authority of the victim and give it to the perpetrator.

i. They empower people to use their power. Rock music, horoscope, fortune telling, etc.

j. They torment people physically, emotionally, and mentally.

k. They control and manipulate against a person's will. They take control of a person's will, mind and emotions, and carry out their work through that person. They cause the person to lie and to believe their own lie.

l. They take inordinate authority, and violate proper authority.

m. Satan has many counterfeits of God's work. He is not original, he does not create anything, and he only copies and perverts what God does.

Some counterfeits that Satan uses:

Satan has the ability to cause supernatural things to occur. He has caused some Christians to admire his supernatural works. He has caused others to be so afraid of the supernatural that they miss the full work of the Holy Spirit.

There are several tests we can use to discern the work of the Holy Spirit from the work of devils and demons. 1 Corinthians 14:33 talks about the spirit of confusion. The Holy Spirit does not perform a circus. He is here to make Jesus real to us. The work of the Holy Spirit always conforms to the Scriptures. The Holy Spirit will always exalt the real Jesus not "another Jesus" (2 Corinthians 11:4). Cults and occults will not admit that Jesus was born of a virgin, that He was God incarnate, was the one and only Son of God and that He was raised from the dead. This is usually the dividing line (1 John 4:2-3).

4. Some examples of deliverance and how demons act.

a. Jesus cast out a devil by a mother's faith (Mark 7:29).

b. The Gadarene demonic was delivered, and the devils went to the hogs (Mark 5:1-20).

c. In Matthew 9:32-33 the dumb spoke after the demon was cast out.

d. In Matthew 10:7 Jesus empowered His disciples to cast out devils.

e. In Mark 9:17-29 the dumb spirit was in the boy from his youth.

f. The Old Testament has types and shadows of how demons operate. Look at Psalms 10, 56, 59, 64 and many others. Other good examples are Old Testament wars, tribes and people, like Jezebel and Balaam. Read these stories and put demons in the roles of Israel's enemies.

5. How they get a foothold in your life.

a. Your sin. All sins give demons a foothold, but one of the worst is sexual sin. Sexual acts bind two people together spiritually in a very unique way.

b. Generational sin. Demons follow families for generations, and have the right to put the same disease and curses on them (the law of inheritance). Demonic religions are based upon worship of ancestral spirits in order to perpetuate curses and control of families. They convince people, even Christians, that they must pay a price to a witch doctor for protection. Some even purchase items and drinks as a way to receive protection and blessings. These people believe that by contacting and being in touch with the spirit of their ancestors that they will be blessed and have protection from evil.

Actually, just the opposite happens. They become prisoners to the enemy of their soul, Satan!

Most festivals like Mardi Gras in America are designed to perpetuate curses over regions. Sometimes even family reunions can be used by demons to perpetuate family curses. Voodoo and other occults all have festivals. Generational curses are the primary and most powerful way that demons attach themselves. Generational spirits often attempt to captivate young members of a family during the teenage years. This is the time when rebellion is most evident. If they cannot succeed, they will try again later in life.

This advice is for those who really want to be free, radically free. Be cautious of well meaning family members who would attempt to control or influence your life, or the life of your children. I can personally testify to this. Be careful that you allow the Holy Spirit, and His ordained authority figures, to control your life and that of your children.

c. Sin in the world. This world is full of sin that promotes demon activity.

d. Weights, or oppression you might receive from someone else. A very common tactic used by demons is to sexually abuse a young person and thus gain entry for the rest of his/her life. A weight is not a sin you performed, rather it is oppression against you by someone else's sin.

e. Through an idol in your life. An idol can be anything that you make more important than God. It can be a person, a habit, a custom, and even a denomination.

f. Rebellion against authority. If a person does not submit to Jesus as Lord, that person, by default, will be under the control of some other being. Satan deceived Eve, and she deceived Adam. Adam should have taken dominion over Satan but he did not. Eve, in effect, took inordinate authority and Adam did not exercise his ordained authority. The original sin demonstrates how authority and sin are so tied together. Obviously, they both should have submitted to the authority of God's Word (the Tree of Life).

g. Christians can be vulnerable. If we have demons before coming to Jesus, there could be a period of time before we receive deliverance. Some never do receive deliverance based upon the fact that they do not wish to totally yield. Obviously a Christian cannot be "possessed" by a demon, but they sure can be influenced. It does not matter if we use the term possessed, influenced, oppressed or whatever. What matters is that we know how to get rid of their activities in our lives.

These Scriptures show that we are still vulnerable even after we believe. "The Spirit clearly says that in later times some will abandon the faith and follow deceiving spirits and things taught by demons" (1 Timothy 4:1). "Be self-controlled and alert. Your enemy the devil prowls around like a roaring lion looking for someone to devour" (1 Peter 5:8). "But I am afraid that just as Eve was deceived by the serpent's cunning, your minds may somehow be led astray from your sincere and pure devotion to Christ. For if someone comes to you and preaches a Jesus other than the Jesus we preached, or if you receive a different spirit from the one you received, or a different gospel from the one you accepted, you put up with it easily enough" (2 Corinthians 11:3,4).

Some say that the blood of Jesus protects Christians. Yes and no. The blood only protects when we are obedient Christians. "...who have been chosen according to the foreknowledge of God the Father, through the sanctifying work of the Spirit, for obedience to Jesus Christ and sprinkling by his blood: Grace and peace be yours in abundance" (1 Peter 1:2). Christians do need deliverance.

6. What you can do.

When Satan convinced Adam and Eve to sin, he gained dominion over them and the human race. He is more powerful than mere humans are. As long as sin is not dealt with, Satan is in charge. Jesus bore our sin at the Cross and paid the final penalty. If we know that truth and practice obedience to it, we will be free from Satan and demons.

Deliverance does not always mean some violent casting out with someone laying hands on us, although that is possible and happens often. There are other ways. We can be delivered ourselves.

a. Be honest. Confess your sin. Practice honesty and truth at all cost. When you lie you make Satan your father.

b. Renounce any contact you have had with anything demonic: music, porno, TV, movies, drugs, alcohol, occult, horoscope, Quija boards, fortune telling, card games, etc.

c. Renounce any relationship to family ties that may be used to pass down curses. We can be courteous to family without receiving their curses.

d. Stay close to Jesus through prayer, His Word, selective friends, and church groups. Keep your mind filled with Godly things. The mind is the battlefield.

e. Be open for however God wants to deliver you. Desire to be free and don't limit God. He has many ways to set you free. His mission is to set you free (Luke 4).

f. Sometimes people get rid of demons and they do not fill themselves up with the Word of God and a holy lifestyle. In many such cases the demons come back in seven times worse. It is important to have Godly counseling after deliverance. "When the unclean spirit has gone out of a man, he walks through dry places seeking rest. And finding none, he says, I will return to my house from which I came out. And when he comes, he finds *it* swept and decorated. And he goes and takes seven other spirits more wicked than himself, and entering in, they dwell there. And the last state of that man is worse than the first" (Luke 11:24-26).

However, there is a safe and practical way to be delivered. The word of Jesus cast out a devil in Matthew 8:16. It can do the same for you. I can personally testify to this method. If you fill up a container before you empty it, there is no danger of having an empty space that can be inhabited with another substance. So also, if you fill yourself up with the Word of God, not only will the demons come out, but there will no empty place left for them to return.

"And evening coming on, they brought to Him many who had been possessed with demons. And He cast out the spirits with a word, and healed all who were sick" (Matthew 8:16). Soaking in the Word will drive demons out of your life.

I would like to invite every reader to now determine to subscribe to this method. Even if you do not believe that you have any problems, you never really know for sure.

Just do this. Determine in your heart to fill yourself with the Word of God to overflowing. Pour the Word in anyway you can do it. Read the Scriptures, listen to tapes, memorize the Word, keep it on your lips, meditate on it day and night. Obey the Word. Do what it says. The Word will cast out every spirit in your life that is not Holy.

g. Be filled with the Holy Spirit so you can have power to overcome (Acts 1:8).

h. Jesus gave us the power and authority to cast out demons (Mark 16:17).

i. We can detect demons in our lives if we stay close to Jesus. Not all evil and sickness is from demons. Physical problems or lifestyle issues can cause sickness. Evil conduct can be our "flesh." However, if any of these problems are left unresolved they can be entry for demons. We should be on the watch for compulsive behavior, habits that we cannot overcome, lusts, fear and oppressive feelings. Do not allow depression to go on without getting help. Do not tolerate feelings of suicide, destruction or murder. Do not hide feelings of homosexuality and inordinate sex, even sex with yourself. Get some help!

7. God destroyed the devil.

What does it mean that God destroyed the devil? How does the blood of Jesus give us power?

"Since the children have flesh and blood, he too shared in their humanity so that by his death he might destroy him who holds the power of death--that is, the devil-- and free those who all their lives were held in slavery by their fear of death" (Hebrews 2:14,15).

"Now if we died with Christ, we believe that we will also live with him. For we know that since Christ was raised from the dead, he cannot die again; death no longer has mastery over him. The death he died, he died to sin once for all; but the life he lives, he lives to God. In the same way, count yourselves dead to sin but alive to God in Christ Jesus" (Romans 6:8-11).

These verses say that Satan was "destroyed." What does that actually mean? He seems to be running around doing a job of destroying others.

Destroy means to render his power ineffective. How did Jesus do that? The devil is still running around destroying others. When Jesus was resurrected, He was the first born of a brand new race. Jesus put a new nature into you when you were born again. This nature is higher than demons and devils. They have already killed the first *race* of Adam, in Jesus on the Cross. Satan and demons have absolutely no authority over this new race, all they can do is lie to us. When Jesus was resurrected, demons had no more power over Him. He put that life into you.

The word destroy is defined in <u>*Strong's Concordance*</u> *as:*
1) to render idle, unemployed, inactivate, inoperative.
1a) to cause a person or thing to have no further efficiency.
1b) to deprive of force, influence, power.

Here is a very absurd example that may help us remember and picture what "destroyed" actually means.
Let's pretend that you are a cat. A big dog, representing Satan, is harassing you, keeping you on the run, and making you hide. He is stealing your food and even tearing at your hide. Finally, this dog kills you.

Then all of the sudden, by some supernatural miracle, you, the cat, are raised from the dead. This time you are no longer a cat, but a lion! Now this same dog comes and looks at you and he runs because he knows you can kill him! The dog has been destroyed (to cause a person or thing to have no further efficiency, to render idle, unemployed, inactivate, inoperative, to deprive of force, influence, power)!

Just imagine now that this dog comes up with a plan. He comes to you and convinces you that you are still a cat and not really a lion. What if the dog could get you to actually act like a cat? That is what the dog Satan does to many Christians.

Just imagine that Jesus was this "cat" that died. Just before He died however, He became "pregnant" with you and me in the Garden of Gethsemane. When He died and was resurrected, He became the firstborn from the dead. When we are born again, we are also lions.

"And he is the head of the body, the church; he is the beginning and the firstborn from among the dead, so that in everything he might have the supremacy" (Colossians 1:18).

We need to stay focused in the Word and on Jesus so that we will keep these truths in our hearts. If we get away from that focus, we will quickly be swept away by the lies of the world and we will become vulnerable.

8. Knowing Jesus is what is important.
"Not everyone who says to me, 'Lord, Lord,' will enter the kingdom of heaven, but only he who does the will of my Father who is in heaven. Many

will say to me on that day, 'Lord, Lord, did we not prophesy in your name, and in your name drive out demons and perform many miracles?' Then I will tell them plainly, 'I never knew you. Away from me, you evildoers!'" (Matthew 7:21-23).

The following was partially taken from "They Shall Expel Demons", page 215, author Derek Prince.[4]

Prayer for deliverance.
"Lord Jesus Christ, I confess that you are my Lord."

1. Personally affirm your faith in Christ. "Lord Jesus Christ, I believe that You are the Son of God and the only way to God - that you died on the cross for my sins and rose again so that I might be forgiven and receive eternal life."

2. Humble yourself. "I renounce all pride and religious self-righteousness and any dignity that does not come from You. I have no claim on Your mercy except that you died in my place."

3. Confess any know sin. "I confess all my sins before You and hold nothing back." (Now list and confess them.)

4. Repent of all sins. "I repent of all my sins. I turn away from them and I turn to You, Lord, for mercy and forgiveness."

5. Forgive all other people. "By a decision of my will, I freely forgive all who have ever harmed or wronged me. I lay down all bitterness, all resentment and all hatred." (Now list and confess them.)

6. Break with the occult and all false religion. "I sever all contact I have ever had with the occult or with all false religion. I renounce all the works of the devil, Satan and other evil spirits in my life. I confess and renounce all my occult practices and sins as abominations before You, a Holy and righteous God. I renounce any occult influence from my forefathers." (Now list and confess them.)

7. Prepare to be released from every curse over your life. "Lord Jesus, I thank You that on the cross You were made a curse, that I might be redeemed from every curse and inherit God's blessing. I renounce every curse from my forefathers. On that basis I ask You to release me and set me free to receive the deliverance I need."

8. Take your stand with God. "I take my stand with You, Lord, against all Satan's demons. I submit to You, Lord, and I resist the devil. Amen!

9. Expel. "Now I speak to any demons that have control over me. (Speak directly to them.) I command you to go from me now. In the name of Jesus, I expel you! I pray that any evil power or ability I may possess, or which have oppressed or possessed me, be completely destroyed or removed from me. I commit myself, my body, my mind, my personality, my emotions, my whole being to the Lord Jesus Christ to be my Lord and savior. I pray this in the mighty Name of Jesus, believing I am delivered."

Chapter 11
Baptism in the Holy Spirit

In Luke 3:16 John the Baptist said, "I baptize you with water, but a mightier one than I is coming and He shall baptize you with the Holy Spirit and fire."

Many believers do not recognize some very key things that Jesus told His disciples in John chapters 14, 15 and 16. He knew that He was to be killed, that He would be resurrected and come back. He also knew that He would leave a second time and that He would send the Holy Spirit to take His place.

He said the following knowing we they could feel fatherless if we could not experience His presence. "I will not leave you as orphans [fatherless]; I will come to you" (John 14:18).

He told His disciples before he ascended that they would be immersed into the Holy Spirit. "For John baptized with water, but in a few days you will be baptized with the Holy Spirit" (Acts 1:5). "But you will receive power when the Holy Spirit comes on you; and you will be my witnesses in Jerusalem, and in all Judea and Samaria, and to the ends of the earth" (Acts 1:8).

He told them not to worry after He left. He explained that the Holy Spirit would take His place and make Him (Jesus, God) real to them. Read what Jesus told them in John 14:16-26.

Jesus told them that the Holy Spirit would make Him real to them. I believe this is the main purpose for the Baptism in the Holy Spirit

"When the Counselor comes, whom I will send to you from the Father, the Spirit of truth who goes out from the Father, he will testify about me" (John 15:26).

"But I tell you the truth: It is for your good that I am going away. Unless I go away, the Counselor will not come to you; but if I go, I will send him to you" (John 16:7).

Jesus told His men that he would come back soon. He did! He came back in the form of the Holy Spirit. The Holy Spirit and Jesus are not different people, they are the same, but in different form. The Holy Spirit can actually dwell inside humans, where Jesus was restricted to one human body.

The disciples had two experiences with the Holy Spirit. The original disciples received the Holy Spirit of the resurrected Christ in John 20:22. However these same men had no visible change of character until they received the Holy Spirit of the ascended Christ on the day of Pentecost in Acts chapter 2.

A. Resurrection Sunday, John 20:22.

Resurrected Christ.
In-breathed Spirit.
Result was life.

B. Pentecost Sunday, Acts 2:4.
   Ascended and Glorified Christ.
   Outpoured Spirit.
   Result was power.

The group of 120 in Acts chapter 2 abandoned themselves, they became lost in the presence of God. There were obedient to Jesus. They spent time and invested words for intimacy. They received power that transformed their lives, power to witness, power to have all their needs supplied, power to expand their influence in other lands and power to experience intimacy and fellowship with the Glorified Christ on a daily basis.

Jesus is no longer the man walking the Sea of Galilee, nor the man suffering on the Cross, nor the man who was simply resurrected. He is now different! No human being saw Jesus in this state, except John on the Isle of Patmos as recorded in the Book of Revelation. Look at Revelation chapter 1.

The disciples experienced something on the day of Pentecost that we all need to experience. When Jesus went back to Heaven the second time in Acts chapter 1, He took a new position as the ascended Christ, not just the resurrected Christ. Jesus left earth in the form of a resurrected being, but He came back through the Holy Spirit as a much superior being, one who had ascended to the right hand of God and who had been glorified.

Notice, His disciples did not mourn in Acts chapters 1-3 as they did in the Book of John when He was crucified. This time, when He left, they took Him at His word of promise that He was coming back soon in another form. Not too many days after He left, He did come back as the Holy Spirit, and they were filled. Then, they proceeded to live their life in fellowship with Jesus just as if He were there with them (He was).

Baptized means to be immersed.
First we are baptized with water and now with fire. The fire is His presence. When we are baptized in water we are (in type) dead, we are humiliated, but the water does not go into us and totally kill us. It is exterior. Baptism in the Holy Spirit is the fire of God going inside us. It is our choice. We can choose our pride over His presence and control over us. He wants to kill our old nature by fire. God promised Noah there would be no more water, but only fire. Demons are destroyed by fire not water.

Do we need to be filled more than once? Some denominations argue about this and miss the whole point. We are not independent containers filled with an outside source, as water from a pitcher being poured into a glass. If this were true, then perhaps we would need to be filled again and again because we have the possibility of leaking.

John 15 says that we are connected to our source like a branch on a vine. It is not a matter of being re-filled, but a matter of staying connected to the vine. The sap in the vine represents the Holy Spirit, Jesus is the vine and we are the branches. We need to abide in the vine. Jesus says that obedience to His Word is what keeps us abiding. The Baptism in the Holy Spirit is being flooded with God when we are connected to Him as the vine and the branch. His sap flows into us, and we stay connected if we abide.

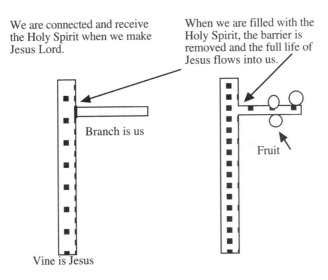

How much filling is enough? Luke 6:45b says, "for of the abundance of the heart his mouth speaketh." Personally, I like the idea that the Holy Spirit flows out of my mouth telling me that I am full!

There has been much confusion and controversy about the Baptism in the Holy Sprit. Some talk about the gifts of the Spirit being the main issue and some talk about tongues being the main issue. Some say baptism is for service, that if we really desire to serve Jesus and witness with power, we need to be filled with the Holy Spirit. They are not wrong, they all have merit, but I do not believe that they touch the primary purpose of the fullness of the Holy Spirit.

What about the gifts of the Spirit?

I feel that we need to leave the giving of gifts to the giver. I have personally had many of the gifts operate in my life from time to time, but not all of them.

I believe in speaking in tongues as a valuable and powerful gift. God uses it not only in public ministry, but more importantly He uses it to take control of our mind for His benefit. James 3:4-5 says that the tongue is like the rudder that guides the entire ship. If you want to give Jesus the rudder of your life, you should give Him your tongue. It will renew your mind, pray the perfect will of God, and resist Satan. Praying in tongues privately for extended periods of time is powerful. It has produced miracles in my life. There is a full teaching on this in the ISOB curriculum called "The Holy Spirit and the tongue."

I do not feel it is proper for people who have received the gifts to make those who have not received them feel as if there is something wrong with them. Neither is it proper for those who have not received the gifts to condemn those who have. Jesus, in Matthew 12:31, said that speaking against what the Holy Spirit is doing is a sure way to never receive those benefits in your own life. Blasphemy of the Holy Spirit is saying something is not of the Holy Spirit when it really is. If you are not sure, that is fine, but be careful never to speak against it unless you are truly sure and have confirmation that it is a counterfeit of Satan. It is better to be safe than sorry!

How can Jesus accomplish all He promised to do for us unless He is real to us? The Holy Spirit makes Jesus real to us so that He perform those things promised in Isaiah 61.

God's wants to set us free from different kinds of slavery. However, the freedom is not the end purpose. The end purpose is to give us freedom so that we may enter into His presence and fellowship with Him, which will result in bearing fruit for our lives and for the Kingdom of God.

1. We are set free from bondage so that.....

2. We may enjoy His Presence and bear fruit.

In the Book of Exodus, God was using Moses to free His people Israel from the slavery of Egypt and Pharaoh. "Let My people go, that they may hold a feast to Me in the wilderness" (Exodus 5:1b). Freedom from Egypt was not the big issue, the main thing with God was the "feast in the wilderness," or in other words, fellowship with Him in His presence.

1. Freedom from bondage.

Jesus quoted Isaiah 61 in Luke 4:18 when He announced His purpose for His ministry. Isaiah 61 starts out with Jesus saying that the Spirit of the Lord has anointed Him to bring good news to the poor, afflicted and broken hearted. Jesus proclaims liberty to the captives, opens prisons for those who are bound, binds up the broken hearted and proclaims the "Acceptable year of the Lord" or "Year of Jubilee" (the time when slaves would go free). He goes on to list many other things that His ministry would accomplish.

He says that these prisoners and poor people would be changed and that they would be trees of righteousness, strong and in right standing with God. He said that they would no longer be heavy with sadness and mourning, but that they would be filled with joy.

Then He said that they would rebuild the waste places. In other words, their wasted lives would be rebuilt, like Nehemiah (whose name means the comforter or the Holy Spirit) rebuilding the broken down walls of Jerusalem. In addition, He said that all their needs would be taken care of and they would become priests of God, or His personal representatives. They would then, in turn, become deliverers and set others free.

Isaiah 61 summarized says that Jesus would convert people from prisoners to priests through the Holy Spirit. This is what we spoke about in Chapter 1 in this book, that we would bear fruit in all three areas of our lives; our character, our needs and our ministry to others. From prisoner to priest.

Isaiah 61:1-7 says,

"1 "The Spirit of the Lord GOD is upon Me, Because the LORD has anointed Me To preach good tidings to the poor; He has sent Me to heal the brokenhearted, To proclaim liberty to the captives, And the opening of the prison to those who are bound;

2 To proclaim the acceptable year of the LORD, And the day of vengeance of our God; To comfort all who mourn,

3 To console those who mourn in Zion, To give them beauty for ashes, The oil of joy for mourning, The garment of praise for the spirit of heaviness; That they may be called trees of righteousness, The planting of the LORD, that He may be glorified."

4 And they shall rebuild the old ruins, They shall raise up the former desolations, And they shall repair the ruined cities, The desolations of many generations.

5 Strangers shall stand and feed your flocks, And the sons of the foreigner Shall be your plowmen and your vinedressers.

6 But you shall be named the priests of the LORD, They shall call you the servants of our God. You shall eat the riches of the Gentiles, And in their glory you shall boast.

7 Instead of your shame you shall have double honor, And instead of confusion they shall rejoice in their portion. Therefore in their land they shall possess double; Everlasting joy shall be theirs."

Jesus promised to do this for all of us, but He is not here on Earth any longer. He sent another comforter, the Holy Spirit, to take His place. The Holy Spirit is the one who now administers this promise to us. We cannot partake of all of these advantages if we are not in touch with Jesus through the Holy Spirit.

We need Jesus to be real to us. We need to be vitally linked with Him in order to experience all that is promised in Isaiah 61. When things are going bad in our lives, if we can hear Jesus speak to us, everything will be all right!

If we are prisoners, if we are poor, broken hearted and beat down, we do not need to wait to go to Heaven for help; we need it NOW! We can have it now in this life, but we need to be in touch with God. He needs to be real to us. He needs to be more than a religion, more than the doctrine of our denomination, more than the words of Scripture (as important as they are). We need to be in touch with the living Jesus in the same way as His disciples were when He was on Earth, and in the same way they were after He left Earth, as in the Book of Acts.

Ephesians 3:18-19 says, "That you may have the power and be strong to apprehend and grasp with all the saints, the experience of that love, what is the breadth and length and height and depth of it, That you may really come to know practically, through experience for yourselves, the love of Christ, which far surpasses mere knowledge without experience: that you may be filled through all your being unto all the fullness of God, may have the richest measure of the divine Presence, and become a body wholly filled and flooded with God Himself."

God became real to Jacob in Genesis chapter 28. Jacob got a taste of God's presence and then could not do without it! Genesis chapter 28 verses 10-17 tells about Jacob's experience with God's presence when he dreamed about the ladder connecting heaven and earth. Jacob arose the next morning early and built an altar there and called it Bethel, the House of God. He was completely captured by intimacy with God. God was real to him. Jacob was like you and me. He needed a lot of change. His flesh nature was corrupt. The only way God could change him, was to lure Jacob to fall in love with Him. God revealed Himself to Jacob. Jacob fell head over heels in love with God, and followed Him the rest of his life. Later, as they walked together, Jacob was finally changed from Jacob to Israel.

When Jesus came into my life, I was truly a spiritual prisoner. There were demons controlling my life. When I saw Jesus in the Book of

Revelation as the ascended Christ, the victor and deliverer, I became a man wholly filled with the Holy Spirit. This occurred on the 26th day of August, 1979. Jesus became as real to me as the man next door. He spoke to me and listened to me. He was with me in my pain and troubles. When people made fun of me, He comforted me. When people tried to keep me captive, He would teach me truths that set me free. Pretty soon, as Isaiah in chapter 10:27 puts it, the anointing made my "neck" so thick that the yoke of oppression could no longer fit on me.

Little by little, Jesus not only set me free from the demons that were influencing me and holding me, but also from the demons that had gained a "home" in me. As I would fellowship with Jesus in the Word and prayer, I would cry uncontrollably, and masses of water and mucus would come out of my body. Luke 11:24 says that the demons come out of a man and wander in dry places, wanting to gain entry in the "wet" place again. The wet place, their original home, is man who is made up mostly of water. This deliverance continued weekly over a period of several months, maybe years, I cannot remember.

As time went on, I became free from the demons that used to hold me captive. My character began conforming to the image of Jesus. My needs began to be provided for. God gave me His choice for a wife and family.

After many years of discipline, He has made me a minister of God, as is promised in Isaiah 61. The agency that God used in this transformation was the Holy Spirit, who made Jesus real to me. Jesus did the work, the Holy Spirit was the agent inside me driving out everything not of God.

2. To enjoy His Presence and bear fruit.

After freedom from slavery, God wants us to experience His presence and His Kingdom. The Holy Spirit makes the Kingdom of God real to us in this life. I encourage you to open your Bible to Hebrews chapter 12 for a study in that chapter.

Notice that the theme Scripture for this Section, Hebrews 12, talks about running the race, but it also talks about getting rid of every weight and sin. "Therefore since we also are surrounded with so great a cloud of witnesses, let us lay aside every weight and the sin which so easily besets *us*, and let us run with patience the race that is set before us" (Hebrews 12:1).

The chapter goes on to talk about the reality of Heavenly Jerusalem, called Mt. Zion the city of the living God (the Kingdom of God). Apparently, getting rid of sin and weights, and going through the rest of the process described in Hebrews 12 has a lot to do with making the Kingdom of God real in our lives.

Let's examine what the writer of Hebrews was saying to these people about running the race, getting free from weights and sin, and the Kingdom of God becoming real to us.

1. In Hebrews 12:2-4 we are told that we must stand with endurance. We must endure criticism, being misunderstood, persecution and standing in patience while Jesus is growing the seed in our heart for fruit.

2. In Hebrews 12:5-11 we are told that God will chastise us, not beat us up, but correct us as sons and daughters with love for our benefit. We truly need the chastisement of God. We have blind spots that we cannot see.

Jacob was a selfish and unruly person. God truly chastised him through circumstances until God changed his name from Jacob to Israel, from trickster to one who prevails with God.

We need to see our circumstances as re-engineered by God so that as we work through them, our character is changed into His likeness. This does not mean that God brings bad circumstances into our life. He does not; Satan does. You can be sure, however, that God uses those circumstances to grow us into His image. God uses His Word to chastise us, but there are areas of our old flesh nature that just have to go through trials to be burned off.

3. In Hebrews 12:12 and 13 we are encouraged to keep going when situations are looking bad.

4. In Hebrews 12:14 we are told to pursue peace and holiness, without which we will not see the Lord, or the Lord will not become real to us.

5. We are told in Hebrews 12:15 to pursue grace and avoid bitterness. We are also told to not be like Esau who lost his birthright and could no longer repent.

6. Now, here is the reward. Read Hebrews 12:18-29. You are come (past tense) to Mt. Zion, a spiritual kingdom, The Kingdom of God. It is in the now, not only in the hereafter. God wants us to live in the heavenly realm, right now, while we are still on Earth. We can actually live in the "next age," the Kingdom Age (Hebrews 6:5), but we need to be filled with the Holy Spirit to experience this. He mentions that Mt. Zion, or the Kingdom of God, has several attributes.

a. First, is the living God. The Holy Spirit enables us to fellowship with the Living God now because He is here with us.

b. Next, is the Heavenly Jerusalem. The Holy Spirit enables us to live in the Kingdom of God, as a reality, now.

c. Then, angels are mentioned. We are not to get too focused on angels, but we need to know that they are here to do battle for us and they move at the Word of God.

d. We have come to the Church of the Firstborn, Jesus, those who are citizens of Heaven. This infers we are to be plugged into a good Bible believing, Spirit filled church.

e. God the Judge is mentioned in verse 23. I am glad that God is my judge, because that makes my savior my judge! He does not condemn, He convicts so that we can repent and win. God is also the judge of our enemy, Satan. He has judged him a loser. God will judge you righteous and judge Satan a loser in every *trial of life.*

f. Hebrews 12:23 mentions the spirits of the redeemed who have gone to Heaven. I do not believe in contacting the spirits of the saints gone before us, but I do believe that they see us. We are viewed and cheered on by the cloud of witnesses. Their testimony of faith is what we see.

g. Hebrews 12:24 tells us that we have Jesus as the Mediator of the blood covenant. Thank God for this. Jesus not only makes the blood covenant with us, but He was raised from the dead to become the mediator, the guarantee of the covenant. When we make mistakes, Jesus takes over until He can get to us to repent and confess our sin. He is our mediator, our advocate. He makes sure we win.

h. In Hebrews 12:25 we are warned to take this process very seriously, for if we neglect or reject this offer we end up in bad shape.

i. In Hebrews 12:26-28 we are told that God is shaking everything in Heaven and Earth, so that those things that need to be removed will be, and those things that are firm and stable, based upon God's Kingdom, will stand the test and stand firm.

j. Finally Hebrews 12:29 tells us that God is a consuming fire. The consuming fire is the Holy Spirit. He comes to deliver us from all that can be shaken, from everything and every residue of the old creation, our flesh and sin nature.

What can we do to cooperate with God?

1. We need to be hungry for God to be real to us. The 120 in the Upper Room were just a small number of people who Jesus had revealed Himself to after the resurrection. There were at least 500. What happened to the others? Perhaps that were not hungry enough. Maybe they were too proud, or too engrossed in their work or their family. Maybe they were too worried what others would think of them. Remember the 120 were criticized and laughed at. The 120 were in unity and one accord.

2. We have to be radical in the Word to be victorious. The blood covenant is cut not by blood but by words. The more Word you have the more blood you have, the more character of Jesus you have, the more sin He removes, the less influence demons have, and the more of the Holy Spirit you have. "For the one whom God has sent speaks the words of God, for God gives the Spirit without limit" (John 3:34).

3. We need to be prepared to be rejected by our family or our denomination. Luke 12:49-52 says, "I have come to bring fire on the earth, and how I wish it were already kindled! But I have a baptism to undergo, and how distressed I am until it is completed! Do you think I came to bring peace on earth? No, I tell you, but division. From now on there will be five in one family divided against each other, three against two and two against three."

4. We need to be open to Jesus and trust Him. Luke 11:11-12 says, "If a son shall ask bread of any of you that is a father, will he give him a stone, or if he ask a fish, will he for a fish give him a serpent? Or if he shall ask an egg, will he offer him a scorpion? If you then, being evil know how to give good gifts unto your children: how much more shall your heavenly father give the Holy Spirit to them that ask Him?"

5. The Holy Spirit always honors repentance. He seems to show up when we turn from our sin, the ways of the world, our pride and our laziness. Acts 26:18 says, "in order to open their eyes so that they may turn from darkness to light, and from the authority of Satan to God, so that they may receive remission of sins and an inheritance among those who are sanctified by faith in Me."

6. We receive the Holy Spirit by faith. Faith in what? Jesus spoke about the fullness of the Holy Spirit in John 7:38-39, "He who believes on Me, as the Scripture has said, 'Out of his belly shall flow rivers of living water.' (But He spoke this about the Spirit, which they who believed on Him should receive; for *the* Holy Spirit was not yet *given*, because Jesus was not yet glorified)."

So Jesus needed to be glorified before we can have faith in receiving the Holy Spirit as an overflow of living water. What does glorified mean? Glorify is a word that means for the true thing to be revealed and disclosed. It is like someone taking a drape off of a new statue and revealing it for the first time.

In John 17:4-5 Jesus was praying to the Father and He said, "I have glorified You upon the earth. I have finished the work which You have given Me to do. And now Father, glorify Me with Yourself with the glory which I had with You before the world was." Jesus revealed the Father to the people with whom He came into contact. Now it was the Father's turn to show who Jesus really was.

How was Jesus glorified? Remember, glorified means to show the true identity of the person or object. In Luke 24:13-27 Jesus is talking to the two men on the road to Emmaus. He said, "'Did not the Christ have to suffer these things and then enter his glory?' And beginning with Moses and all the Prophets, he explained to them what was said in all the Scriptures concerning himself" (Luke 24:26,27). Then these two men got so excited that they found the 11 disciples and they began to tell them what Jesus had just revealed. All of the sudden the resurrected Jesus showed up at this meeting and took over. "He said to them, 'This is what I told you while I was still with you: Everything must be fulfilled that is written about me in the Law of Moses, the Prophets and the Psalms.' Then he opened their minds so they could understand the Scriptures. He told them, 'This is what is written: The Christ will suffer and rise from the dead on the third day'" (Luke 24:44-46).

He gave them revelation or glorified Himself in Moses, Psalms and the Prophets. It says in verse 45 in the Amplified version, "He thoroughly opened up their minds to the Scriptures." He was speaking about the Five books of Moses, the Books of the Prophets and the Psalms.

Shortly after this, Pentecost took place and they were baptized in the Holy Spirit and fire!

He glorified Himself in Moses:

In Genesis as the creator and the seed of woman. He showed Himself to be the propagator of a new race through a blood covenant to replace the fallen race of Adam.

In Exodus, He showed Himself as the lawgiver and as the Passover Lamb for the broken law. He is the one who splits the Red Seas of our lives freeing us from the bondages of the world.

In Leviticus, He is the maker of the blood covenant, and the one who asks that we take up our cross and live in holiness.

In Numbers, He is our provider in the deserts of our life; He is our manna from Heaven and our water from the rock.

In Deuteronomy, He is the one who redeems us from the curse of the law.

He glorified Himself in The Psalms:

In Psalms, He is our shepherd and the one to whom we can pour out all of the troubles of our heart in honesty and without condemnation, like David did.

He glorified Himself in The Prophets:

In Isaiah He is the suffering Saviour who takes our sin and sickness.

In Joel, He shows the promise of the baptism in the Holy Spirit. However, before the promise in Joel chapter 2, He showed the required consecration which precedes the promise.

He also showed them what I saw when I got saved and filled at the same time in the Book of Revelation as it is foreshadowed in Ezekiel and Daniel.

In Ezekiel 37, He is the one who gives our dry bones the new birth with the Holy Spirit. In chapters 38-39, He defeats our enemies. In chapters 40-42, He shows us the temple of God so that we will know that we are invited to get into a close relationship with Him.

In Ezekiel 43, He showed them the glory of the throne and the tabernacle where God meets man as in Revelation 21. In Chapter 44-46, He asks us to consecrate ourselves so that we may be baptized in the Holy Spirit.

In Ezekiel 47, as in Revelation 22, He is the one who baptizes with the Holy Spirit which causes the river to flow out of our innermost beings into the dead sea of humanity so that people can be made alive with God.

In Ezekiel 48:35 His name is "the Lord is there," in the heavenly Jerusalem dwelling with His people.

In Daniel chapters 1-6, He reveals Himself as the one who asks us to be in the world but not of the world. He is with us in the fiery furnaces and lion dens of our lives.

In Daniel chapter 7, He shows Himself as the Ancient of days who gave kingdom victory to the saints. In chapters 8-9 the battles are likened to the battles in Revelation.

In Daniel 10:5, He shows the ascended victorious Christ as in Revelation. Chapters 10 and 11 shows more war.

Daniel 12 tells about the need to stand, for the enemy will wear out some. Now look at Daniel 12:12. For those who stand to the end, there will be victory. This is what I saw when I got saved and filled with the Holy Spirit at the same time in 1979!

In the New Testament, Jesus truly revealed Himself as the Lamb of God who takes away the sin of the world. He resolved the paradoxes of the Old Testament that said that God is merciful and forgives sin, yet visits the inequities upon the children of up to four generations (Exodus 34:6-7).

He revealed Himself as the Son of God, as the Word of God, as the Truth, the Life and the Way!

He revealed Himself as the Messiah who will come back a second time as a great King on the throne.

In John 14-16, He revealed Himself as the Holy Spirit who would live in His disciples.

In Luke 24 and Acts 1 Jesus told His disciples to consecrate their lives and go and tarry or wait until the promise came. This is our part: obedience, consecration and abandonment.

Prayer. Lord Jesus, the Word of God says that you have a desire to fill me with your Spirit so that You and I can be more intimate. I am hungry for you and your presence in my life. Jesus, I believe your Word. I confess to you that I want everything you have for me. Come, Jesus, baptize me with the Holy Spirit and fire. I am open and ready for the fire in my life. I renounce and repent from all sin in my life. I forgive everyone who has wronged me. I offer myself to you a living sacrifice. You are sovereign over my life. Have your way. I offer to you all of my members, my mouth, my tongue, my hands, feet, ears and eyes.

Take it all!

Student Feedback Form

Name _____ Date:

_____

Book _____ Chapter (s) #

_____

1.   Write here what stood out to you the most in this chapter.

2.   Write here what, if anything, you feel that God wants you to do or
      obey in this chapter. In other words, what do you feel you need to
      do now that you have read this chapter?

3.   What in this chapter would you like to understand better. Do you
      have any questions that you feel need to be answered? Write down
      your questions here.

4.   Write here a prayer you would like us to pray with you in
      agreement.

Appendix A - List of ISOB Lessons

List of ISOB Lessons available on CD ROM for Windows and Apple computers. These lessons are also available on our web site http://www.isob-bible.org/

Grow or Die book
01 Grow or Die Bearing Fruit
02 Prisoners in the Promise Land
03 The Flowing River - (to be continued on a regular basis.)
04 Who God Is
05 Sit
06 Walk
07 Stand
• Grow or Die book Section 2 (Blood and Fire)
08. Power to Run the Race
09. The Cross
10. Deliverance- Demons
11. Baptism in Holy Sprit

Who God Is
01 Getting to know our awesome God
02 The Trinity
03 God The Father
04 God The Father - 2
05 God is a covenant person
06 The Virgin Birth
07 The Virgin Birth - 2
08 Who is Jesus Now?
09 Disguises of God
10 God The Word
11 The Authority of God's Word
12 The Integrity of The Word
13 The Purifying Effect of God's Word
14 Christ The Rock
15 Bible Prophecy - Name of Jesus in the Old Testament
16 God The Holy Spirit

17 The Holy Spirit and the Tongue
18 Baptism in the Holy Spirit

Sit

Individual Lessons:

01 Sit Outline - Sitting With Christ
02 Grace
03 Identity
04 Extravagant Love
05 Purchased from Slavery
06 Redemption
07 Who told you?
08 Healing for our Bodies
09 Roots
10 Victory over Sin
11 Fear
12 Guilt
13 Power to Finish the Race - The Cross
14. Enter His Rest.

Walk

01 Walk outline
02 Backsliding
03 Rich Young - consecration
04 Too busy for God
05 Faith
06 Forgive
07 The world
08 Truth/Zakah
09 Truth death penalty
10 Truth
11 Authority
12 Repent
13 Bible Reading
14 Habits for Heaven
15 See the invisible
16 Servanthood
17 Putting others first
18 Honor with your body

Inner Healing
This Series is also called ISOB Bondage Breakers and is presented on 15 videos available on DVD.

1 - A vision to be healed on the inside. -
2 - Rejection ... but "The Father tenderly loves you."
3 - Why does God release you from Bondage?
4 - Grieving - a deeper level of being honest and real.
5 You cannot be free without the Word.
6 You can't be free if you don't know who you are!
7 You can't be free if you don't live like who you really are.
8 You can't be free if you don't know about Satan's tactics.
9 Forgiveness The Inner Healing Ointment
10 You Can't be Free if You Don't Live by Faith.
11 Judgments
12 Soul Ties
13 Scabs, Scars, Success
14 Low Self Esteem and the Importance of a Goal
15 The Purpose of Life

Breaking Free
01 Breaking Free
02 Giants
03 Truth
04 Sorrow
05 Witchcraft
06 Unashamed
07 Turn from the Flesh
08 Reconciliation of Evil 1
09 Reconciliation of Evil 2
10 Reconciliation of Evil 3
11 Authority
12 Testing
13 Visions
14 Ministry
15 Torture
16 Book of John & Proverbs

International School of The Bible Marietta, GA. U.S.A. (770) 565-8736 growordie@isob-bible.org

134

End Notes

(¹) Nee, Watchman. Sit, Walk, Stand. Wheaton, IL: Tyndale House, 1977

(²) The New Strong's Exhaustive Concordance of the Bible. Nashville, TN: Thomas Nelson Publisher, 1995

(³) Vine, W.E. Vine's Complete Expository Dictionary. Atlanta, GA: Thomas Nelson Publishers, 1996

(⁴) Prince, Derek. They Shall Expel Demons. Grand Rapids, MI: Chosen Books, 1998

(⁵) Wurbrand, Richard. Reaching Toward The Heights. Bartlesville, OK: Living Sacrifice Book Company, 1979

(⁶) Nee, Watchman. God's Plan and The Overcomers. Wheaton, IL: Tyndale House, 1979

(⁶) Nee, Watchman. A Table in the Wilderness. Wheaton, IL: Tyndale House, 1965

Notes

Notes

Notes

Notes

Notes

Notes

Notes

Notes

Notes